A WEST AFRICAN ENTREPRENEUR'S CHALLENGING PATH TO FINANCIAL FREEDOM

Ike Onyema Obi
and Janine de Nysschen

A WEST AFRICAN ENTREPRENEUR'S CHALLENGING PATH TO FINANCIAL FREEDOM

For Future and Family

The Emergent Entrepreneur Collection

Collection Editor
Dr Drew Harris

LPp

This memoir is dedicated to my sons, Martin Obinna Ike, and Prince-Nuamah Obi Ike. May it serve as an investment story of how my past has created opportunities for our family and helped to build their future.

First published in 2024 by Lived Places Publishing.

British Library Cataloguing in Publication Data
A CIP record for this book is available from the British Library

ISBN: 9781916704701 (pbk)
ISBN: 9781916704725 (ePDF)
ISBN: 9781916704718 (ePUB)

Cover design by Fiachra McCarthy
Book design by Rachel Trolove of Twin Trail Design
Typeset by Newgen Publishing UK

Lived Places Publishing
Long Island
New York 11789

www.livedplacespublishing.com

Abstract

Ike Onyema Obi recounts his entrepreneurial journey from Nigeria to Ghana and beyond, with its sacrifices and hard choices, that has led him to financial success and secured a better future for himself, his family, and others. Ike's relentless focus on financial freedom and building wealth has been driven by an avid ability to solve problems and seize opportunities, while balancing risk with consistent strategies for investing in his future.

Keywords

African entrepreneurship, Nigeria, Ghana, poverty, homelessness, informal business sector, socio-economic hardship, global diversity, market opportunity financial freedom.

Contents

Introduction

Entrepreneurs the world over share similar traits: they are driven, persistent, and resilient in pursuit of their business goals. Often, the context in which an entrepreneur finds him or herself serves as the catalyst for each one's business journey. Africa has many problems, and those problems helped Ike Onyema Obi become a successful entrepreneur. Perhaps not conventionally. His early life of poverty and limited choices gave Ike what he considers as an unfair advantage. Struggling fuelled his mission to have a future where his family would enjoy freedom from hardship. The moment Ike decided to have a better future, his approach to life became one of short-term sacrifice for long-term gain. Even if that meant enduring homelessness and hunger so that he could save to start a business. Like many young Africans, Ike's search for something better took him away from his home country. Ike left Nigeria for Ghana, pursuing a dream of finding wealth in the Jubilee oil fields. When his plans failed, his future-family-freedom instincts survived. This book tells the many stories of how Ike went from walking the streets of Accra, Ghana, to launching businesses in waste management, always investing in himself and his future. It reflects that Ike's success as an African entrepreneur has come from making sacrifices, understanding money, and solving problems.

Learning objectives

- Learning objective one: to develop an understanding of how context shapes entrepreneurial outcomes. By reading this book, readers will gain insights into the African context, where regulations and standards are sometimes loose and flexible concepts. Readers can explore Ike's willingness to "do before asking permission" and discover how people, often strangers, help him deal with his working outside of regulations, as he builds his business skills.

- Learning objective two: to explore the entrepreneurial mindset that Ike displays, born out of hardship, and shaped instinctively around seeing opportunities and finding ways to solve problems. By reading this book, readers will see the principle of necessity driving invention and innovation in action.

- Learning objective three: to reflect on the extreme effort and personal dedication that it takes to create entrepreneurial success when resources are limited. Readers will discover how Ike turns to books – a cheap resource – and teaches himself to crave understanding. They will notice the amount of reading Ike does even as he struggles to feed himself because he sees book learning as an investment in his future.

- Learning objective four: to become more acquainted with the diversity of Africa, even within the West Africa region. Ike's journey takes him to Anglophone and Francophone environments in West Africa. He is exposed to foreign nationals and multinational expats. By reading about his experiences, readers will be exposed to prejudices between people who may look similar but have different ethnic, tribal, national, and religious backgrounds. Also, to the nuances of relationships between Africans and other national identities.

1
Shaping a new mindset out of poverty

It is early evening in a hot, humid Accra, and I hear my son's laughter echo lightly through the hall of our modern townhome. I pause at the doorway and look down at my wife, kneeling beside the bathtub, stirring up bubbles as my three-year-old giggles with unbound joy. What a treasure, I think, to have light at the flick of a switch, and water spilling freely from a faucet. In that moment, the priceless smile on my son's face makes me happy. Yet my mind immediately wanders to the cost of my family's ongoing happiness. I know the value and reward that comes from suffering and sacrifice to make a good life. Even though I fear letting my children go through any hardship, I would not give up my life's experiences for any amount of money. My only concern is that my past may make me focus on the future without much thought for these present moments. So, I lean forward and scatter some bubbles in the air, laughing with my son, and I say a silent thanks to God, who has been good to me in all ways I can measure.

Today's life in Ghana is far removed from my childhood in Nigeria. My journey to greater financial freedom, having a happy family, and securing a better future, started in one of Port Harcourt's many compounds, where I lived with my parents Eugene and Theresa Ijeoma, and five siblings. It was an interesting place to grow up. The crowded compound we shared with over 40 other families was busy and noisy and lively with children. There were all types of people, some lazy, some abusive, others finding small means to make a living – a place where I never saw anyone who rose above the circumstances. It was a daily struggle and grind. I look back on it as a beautiful childhood in a difficult environment. Everyone was dirt poor, yet there was a richness of community.

To be honest, growing up I never knew we were poor. Everyone lived in the same way. Our homes consisted of one bedroom chamber where our parents would sleep, and a living hall, where they would rearrange chairs at night to make space for the children's sleeping mats. Privacy and hygiene were luxuries I did not know. We shared seven toilets and baths between all the many compound families. Early in the morning there was always a rush. We had to get up before dawn to queue in long lines for the baths. In Nigeria, public water doesn't flow continuously – whenever it was flowing, everyone would have to fill their barrel drums and buckets. If the pipes were dry, there were privately owned boreholes where we would have to buy water for use in our homes, and pure water merchants when we needed drinking water.

Family life flowed amid the difficulties of living. There was the religious fervor of early morning family devotionals, with prayers for our daily blessings and utterances of casting out the devil who caused all suffering. By late afternoon, the hot air would filter the sounds of tired husbands and worn wives fighting and quarreling over petty issues, and of carefree children returning from school to play between the ramshackle dwellings. Children who misbehaved would be disciplined by the adults present in the compound, and if you did something wrong, you could be sure that when your own parents returned, they would be told of your transgressions, and you would face punishment again. For the most part, there was no electricity – but on rare evenings when we had lights, you would see all the children running and jumping around, being happy. Later at night we would all make our way back to our respective homes, and mostly we would take our sleep mats and lie outside in the dark.

My family was of the Igbo tribe, and Igbo families were the businesspeople in the community. My father dealt in the clothes trade, while my mother sold popular garri, a foodstuff made from cassava. Traditionally in Nigeria, the Igbo people are seen to have a culture of industriousness. I take my creative and enterprising roots from this rich tribal heritage. Education is also valued in Nigeria, and the schools I attended in junior and senior years were around and near our compound, so I did not have to become a boarder. For schooling in general, children entered the system around the age of six – there was no kindergarten back then, unless one showed brilliance, and you would start schooling at a younger age.

My very first school, Banham Memorial Primary, was located on Aggrey Road, one of the major routes through Old Township District, which bustled with trading and retail activity. Even though the ratio of pupils to teachers was about fifty to one, I recall that we each had our own desk. I was not a top student, but I was diligent. I moved on to secondary level, at Government

Comprehensive Secondary School, which was in my Borokiri neighborhood. The boarding and day school had been set up in 1962 with US support, and it offered a good level of education. One thing I remember is cutting grass at the school. There was a lot of greenery and students were given a Labor Day for manual garden work, or as punishment for arriving late, you would cut grass. Football (soccer) was also a big pastime at the school, and we had two sports fields.

I enjoyed learning and had a good time during my secondary school years. My love of reading was just starting, and it was the time when someone at school introduced me to the book by Napoleon Hill, *Think and Grow Rich*. It may seem a small thing, but to a young boy who has grown up in a place where poverty appears inevitable, this book was life changing. It shaped and molded my new view of what my future could be like – a future that depended on me having an incredible, unshakeable belief in myself and in my goals. Little did I know it then, but Napoleon Hill's principles were the seeds that started me questioning how I could free myself up to create a better future.

The idea that thoughts can make things, irrespective of what is going on around you, has served me well in my entrepreneurial journey. It got to the point where I was so full of the vision and clear on the goals of where I was going – focused on the future I was creating with my thoughts – that even though my suffering increased and as life became more difficult, that hardship felt less. I constantly bombarded my thoughts with what I wanted in my life – I literally structured my mind around being future-motivated regardless of my circumstances, and it's how my head works today.

A lot was said in the book, and now that I am older, I would perhaps see that Hill's approach was a bit intense. Yet I can also look back on my life and recall the great difficulties and challenges I had to surmount, and when I ponder how I overcame the odds, I always come back to the motivational principles of *Think and Grow Rich*, and some of the earliest books that I read, which altered my thinking, and ultimately influenced my actions and decisions. I remember printing out my financial freedom spreadsheet and pinning it to my wall where I could see it every day, and then being so motivated to achieve the goal of freedom that I would walk all the way to the bank on the days I was going to make an investment transaction, because walking instead of taking transport meant I could save a little bit more money.

One good thing about suffering during life is that it has made investment come more naturally to me. I find it easier to invest in buying books, in educating my mind and in building real estate developments, than spending on material goods that are fleeting in value. I don't even know my clothing size because shopping does not motivate me. The desire to move beyond hardship and struggle has been overtaken by a relentless motivation to achieve a better future, with a freedom that will endure.

My life, since my childhood in Port Harcourt, has changed drastically. Recently I completed my new office space, and it seemed beyond belief that my small business could have such a beautiful space. If my sons would only know all the years I spent living in a single hall and chamber, working long hours in a cramped space with only a plastic table and chair for my office, skipping lunch if it meant I could save some money. All that while, I was moving forward, even when it seemed my business was standing still. Because I was building the foundations of my future and creating the freedom for the family I had dreamed about.

As an entrepreneur I have always looked forward to reaching a point where my passive income far exceeds my earned income. A time where I have all the financial stability to do anything I want to do, with my family by my side. Writing this book is about pausing in the moment, so that I do not take it all for granted. My two young sons are living the life I dreamed for them and imagined for my future, birthed by business ideas, a willingness to risk and sacrifice, and persistent motivation. In sharing my entrepreneurial journey, I am creating the story my two sons will one day read to connect them with my past. It is also an investment in the present, to make time to enjoy what I have now. And as always, this book will serve a future purpose too, taking me down a new path with bigger different dreams and goals – because, in the words of Napoleon Hill, I can make my life what I want it to be.

2
Finding Mr Smith and the study boys

When I was in Senior Secondary School (SS2), I had a friend in class, Diepiriye Prabo, and he was always doing well in math, with very good grades. I wondered how he was getting such good math results, because we were both receiving the same level and amount of instruction. We stayed in the same area and when I went home, I would see him going to his house too. But somehow the guy seemed to do well each time we had our math classes. Curious, I spoke to him at school, and asked him whether he was doing extra work, learning on his own at home to be able to perform so well. Diepiriye shared with me that he was being taught math by a Canadian man. Apparently, he was living with a teacher, named Smith. I declared my intention to join these math classes too, and my friend was hesitant. Diepiriye said he wasn't sure how he would introduce me to Smith because it was a special arrangement he had, one that came about because his older brother had also lived and studied with Smith before. Disappointed, all I could do was say that it was okay.

The first day after Diepiriye told me passed, the second day passed, and on the third day, I made up my mind to do something. I waited until after class and carefully watched where my friend was going, trailing him quietly at a distance. We got to the house where he lived with this Mr Smith. I remember there were a lot of well-trimmed fruit trees – mangoes, avocados, oranges, and palm nuts. I peered over the wall and saw it was an old colonial bungalow with discolored glass windows. Other than the lawn that was well-kept, the place looked neglected and in need of a fresh coat of paint. The entry door on the porch had old-fashioned leaded glass panes, and I walked toward it and simply stood waiting in front of the house.

Luckily, Mr Smith was sitting in his living hall, and he looked out and saw me. He called out "Hello gentleman, how can I help you?" He could tell I was a student from my white school shirt and blue shorts. Smith, who was likely in his early fifties, was one of the biggest men I had ever seen – vast and tall. I responded directly, "I am not doing well in math and my friend is, and apparently it has something to do with you." Smith looked at me long and hard – I know my face was filled with the determination I felt in my heart. Getting good math grades was important for my future, and this large white man in his tumbledown government house with its big rooms and laden bookshelves and mismatched tiles and paint peeling off the wall; Mr Smith was the answer.

Smith agreed to teach me mathematics, but he had a set of firm rules. I had to come to his class directly after school every day, and I was not allowed to be late. He said if he detected at any point that I was not serious about the work he set for me, I would be told to leave the group. Sacrificing my afternoons seemed a small price compared to what I believed I would gain, and I told Smith I really wanted to learn. Smith said my mother should buy me a notebook to bring to his class. The following day I got there; it was such a struggle. I was feeling anxious, I was feeling hungry, and I watched as five other boys enthusiastically tackled the work Smith had given them. I looked repeatedly at the quiz paper he had set before me, and I did not know how to do the math. I couldn't answer any of the questions! This made me feel even more nervous, especially when Smith came over and picked up my blank answer sheet.

It was at that moment Smith looked down at me, saw my fear, and said calmly that I should not worry because he knew what to do. And so, he started my lessons with the very basic math functions that I needed to learn. He showed me using an old standard math textbook, which one doesn't really find these days. It was a great textbook with hundreds of questions. There was no way you would finish the exercises for each math segment without learning and understanding the math premises that were being taught.

Smith's math classes became like a religion to me. Every day at 2:30 pm, I would be there to start my lessons. In fact, I loved going to Smith's house to learn. I would stay there until 7 pm most evenings. There was a big table in the main hall, and we could squeeze up to eight boys around it. Even though we were a group of similar-aged students, we seldom talked. Each one focused on his math paper and that is all we did, solve math problems, learn, and solve more complicated math problems. Occasionally Smith would host foreign students, and there would be some interaction. But mostly, it was a sole learning endeavor.

Initially I didn't eat at Smith's house. But I ignored the hunger pangs because I could see myself growing and learning all the time, getting better and better at doing math equations. As for Smith's method of teaching, it was show one, do one. He would present a math problem, then show me the steps he used to solve it. Then he would assign similar problems to solve from his stack of math textbooks. Typically, he would give us each a set of fifty questions to answer and would come afterwards to mark our progress and explain his corrections. It was an excellent period of personal development for me because I had found direction and structure. It did not matter that I was hungry because I felt there was a greater reward – a better future.

As time went by, the study boys would call me to join in the meals, and Smith's house became a part of my daily routine. It was obvious that Smith was not wealthy. Aside from the house being poorly maintained, there was no generator, and the covered carport stood empty (the only times this spot was used was for storing stuff, or when the boys had lady friends who visited, it was a good place for a mattress). But Smith and the rest of the study boys became my safe space. I became a stranger to my family, only spending Saturdays and Sundays at home with my parents. The rest of my time was taken by school, which started at 5 am, and being at Smith's house until late evening, returning home only to remove my school uniform and sleep. By the time I stepped into my family home, my parents would have eaten and were making ready for bed. I hardly saw my siblings.

It got to a point where I saw Smith and the study boys as my real home. And so, I asked Smith if I could move to his house, and he agreed. My mother negotiated the terms with him, that I would stay under Smith's roof, but that I would contribute to his household by being responsible for a good share of chores. That's how I ended up becoming part of Smith's household, sweeping floors, cleaning dishes, and helping around the property for my upkeep. I remember picking huge juicy grapefruit (as I called them, "big oranges that were sour") off the trees, cutting them open and eating them with a spoon, and I still enjoy the tangy sour-sweetness of grapefruit today.

I have clear recollections of Smith reading his *Economist* newspaper every single evening, cup of tea in hand, and seldom wearing more than his T-shirt and a cloth wrap – with long trousers on occasion. I rarely saw him drink, perhaps a Heineken beer occasionally. He loved macaroni and stew! He ate it all the time. Even though he had lived in Nigeria for a long time, he wasn't a fan of our local foods.

Smith introduced me to the world of mathematics, and it fascinated me so much that most of my teenage years I spent buried in textbooks and studies. Eventually I had difficulty conversing with my peers at school and home, because all I thought about was solving math problems, and I had nothing else to talk about to my age-mates. There was no time for girlfriends or socializing. Indeed, by the end of my senior secondary school years, I had worked my way through all of Smith's basic math books, moved on to applied mathematics and then even engineering math. At one point, Smith paid for me to attend private technical drawing classes so that I could gain a foundational understanding of engineering. He purchased the scale ruler, the drawing set squares, the compass, and divider – everything I needed for the class.

Looking back, Smith invested more in me than anyone I know – he was more invested in my future than my own father, or my uncles, after my father passed. He gave me a roof over my head, he put food on the table, and he even paid out of his own pocket for me to attend extra classes. There were six of us living and studying with Smith in my time there. Stanley and Diepiriye were like his wards – he paid all their school fees. Two of the others, Kito and Amilton, were less serious about their studies, and would often take advantage of Smith's good nature by asking him to pay for certain things, and then inflating the prices with their "top-up" share. Still, they were very handy in the home, going to the market, doing most of the cooking, and generally taking care of household things for Smith. Mark was also one of the boys, but it was clear he didn't want to further his life with studies (he eventually became a taxi driver) – Smith's schooling was not important to him. Diepiriye moved to the UK with his wife, and I believe he became an engineer, and Stanley remained in Nigeria to become an accountant.

There's no doubt that Smith's personal life suffered in some ways having us under his roof. Smith had a girlfriend, Jennifer, who lived with us for a while, but the study boys did not welcome her presence. I remember she changed the menu, and she tried to impose a different structure to our communal lifestyle. One time she cooked a big pot of meat stew, and some of the boys came and took a huge chunk out of it before the meal was to be served. She was furious and Smith ended up shouting at us, and it looked like he was going to have a heart attack with all the stress of it. Having a woman in the house disrupted the way we boys organized our lives, and we made it uncomfortable for her to stay.

Living with Smith was a strange contrast to how my mother managed our family household money. Smith was being paid a teacher's salary each month that exceeded my mother's earnings. Yet he would keep on giving his money out until there was nothing, sometimes he would run short by the last week of the month. When I observed my mother, she would carefully plan and manage all her resources and materials to last, and she would always have money to pay her children's school fees. I knew I didn't want to be like Smith in money matters. Perhaps it was these money troubles that made me more conscious of lessons I would read about investing for the future and building wealth. I wouldn't advise anyone to depend on pension – whether you are an entrepreneur or salaried, your money focus should always be on meeting your future needs too. My mother has great respect for Smith; she sends me news of him whenever she crosses paths with his partner Jennifer. It is through her that I am aware of Smith's struggles.

One year I visited Nigeria and discovered that Smith was seriously ill, so I called all the study boys and told them we needed to contribute to Smith's care. Some money came, but one of the boys declined to help, saying Smith should have made his own provision for his old age. That's when I realized that in life, no matter how many people you help, in the end you are on your own. I have resolved not to be dependent on the goodwill of my children; rather to ensure I am able to take care of my own future and to be happy if they do help in some way. It grieves me to see how Smith is going through what he is experiencing now, given the number of students who passed through his classroom when he was a teacher, and the others who benefited from his extra classes and even care in his home.

Aside from the math lessons that Smith taught me, there were life lessons I learned during that time too. For example, I know

now that no matter how bad you are at something, if you work at it persistently and consistently, you will become good at it. That happened to me with mathematics. I also learned from Smith that you don't need to know someone to be willing to help them. Smith never even knew my parents when he offered to teach me, and later to take me in. He never took a single naira from my parents for my board and tuition. He was very trusting too – he would leave his room open and expected us to be honest. Smith was truly a profoundly giving man who cared less for his own welfare than he did for helping us.

I once asked Smith how he came to be in Nigeria, and he told me that after completing his PhD in Canada, he was perplexed by the fact that a country like Nigeria which had a big wealth of oil reserves, would be having difficulty with developing its economy. He told me that one should never underestimate someone who has passion and who is in search of answers. Looking back, I realize that Smith had very good insights into Nigerian issues – problems with electricity, road infrastructure, political strife, etc. There was a point in time when many of Smith's former school students were taking up senior government positions as Directors-General of various departments. But for some of the home study group, I don't think much has resulted in the life of Mark, Amilton, and Kito – they became house boys, and the last time I saw them, it seemed their lives were hard. Stanley, Diepiriye, and I are among those whose lives were transformed through Smith's teaching and unconditional mentoring.

Smith himself had no desire to return to Canada and made little effort to stay in touch with his family there. One time he had an accident and fell and injured his arm badly, with severe fractures to his hand that couldn't be treated properly in Nigeria. I was surprised at the speed with which the Canadian Embassy contacted his relatives, and they flew him back to Canada for treatment almost immediately. He went, and we thought he would not return, but Smith came straight back to us again. His decision to stay in Nigeria into his retirement years has not benefitted him. Even though Smith served the Nigerian Government well in his teaching capacity and nurtured and mentored hundreds of young Nigerians during his years of service and teaching, he has struggled to get a pension allowance in Nigeria. He was never a man to complain, and the only thing I have heard him express frustration about in these past few years is how he is struggling to get Nigerian citizenship despite countless trips to government offices in the capital city, Abuja.

Being with Smith and seeing how difficult his life became shortly after he retired really boggled my mind. He was not paying rent all those years, because his house was a government bungalow. That's why I believe you need to plan for the end of how you will live out your life from a youthful age. I want to be responsible for my own health. I don't want to end up sick and dependent on others out of the goodness of their hearts. I feel that there were indirect lessons I learned from my mother too, that serve me well as an entrepreneur and family man, and that she deserves my gracious respect. Her quiet example of saving money, investing the little she had, paying attention to her business, watching it grow – these lessons were probably more valuable in life than becoming a mathematician or PhD holder. Learning the skills to survive is as important as learning the skills to be productive in one period of life or another. Those early books and watching the contrast between intelligent Smith and my streetwise mother, have shaped my thoughts. As much as I will invest in people, it will not be at the expense of not investing in my own upkeep for the future.

Personally, I believe there is a law of reciprocity. Sometimes I work so hard now because I know I cannot wait until I get to the time when I become fully responsible for taking care of my mother, Smith, and of Papa Amara who also played a pivotal role in shaping my future. Papa Amara bought me my first physics textbook, which opened my mind in new ways, and inspired me to become an engineer.

Sadly, now that Smith is old, poor, and sickly, his former students seldom even ask how he is doing. I stay in touch and visit when I can, sending food parcels and paying medical bills – even though Smith has never once asked for my help. It's a wonder why a man would choose such a life and give and give generously without asking for anything in return. I don't feel it is my place to criticize the life that Smith chose, even in his current hardship. Smith had a huge impact on how my life has turned out, and in gratitude my only return can be to make his path easier where and when I can. My focus remains fixed on always creating a better future for myself and my family. It would be foolish for me to not try to understand a man whose focus was to help create a better future for my country, Nigeria.

3
Seeing my father's fortunes and failures

My father was one of my first entrepreneur mentors, at least as I understood business at the time. In my childhood years, he had a clothing shop that sold mostly imported Chinese men's outfits. My dad's small commercial venture was not uncommon, especially as West Africa's homegrown textile industries began waning. His business was part of the growing Chinese-Nigerian trade, and instead of local fabric, my father sold ready-made imported quality outfits. Before the 1980s, Nigeria was yet to see an influx of Chinese-made clothes, or the vast dumping of second-hand Western clothing. Back then, men and women would find their favorite tailors and seamstresses and would put a lot of thought into choosing their brightly patterned African fabrics and ever-changing outfit styles. If you visited a Nigerian open-air market, you would be overwhelmed by the vibrant energy of bustling buyers and haggling vendors, with their many laden tables crammed under dusty umbrellas. Clothes, car parts, foodstuffs – the markets were a place to find anything and everything, jumbled together.

Armed only with sewing machines, those early Nigerian tailors – perhaps this is true of all tailors – would need to manage customer dynamics with some finesse. In part because clients would have bold demands or would not truly know what they wanted. Tailors would walk the line of confidently assuring potential clients they were experts in a particular style, even if they had never cut or sewn that style before. Every garment would be measured, and custom made, and while one always guaranteed the perfect fit, a good tailor would know how to smooth over inevitable disappointments. Pricing one's tailoring services was also a carefully considered art form. New clients would be charged according to what it looked like they could afford, while repeat clients would be rewarded with discounts and lavish praise.

My father was of the newer generation of Nigerian clothes sellers. His shop was situated in one of River State's emerging formal market zones, where you could still find anything and everything, except now the unruly open-air market stalls had been organized into constructed rows of shops. When this New Market opened in Borokiri, my parents bought a shop, and paid a monthly fee for collective services such as security and cleaning. Unlike the informal markets that traded late into the night, New Market opened at 6 am and closed at 6 pm – that was the fixed time when the security men would unlock the big market access gates, and shopkeepers would start and end their day.

My dad's shop premise was tucked into a row of similar market shops that all made or sold clothing. Every morning my father would set his shop display up to entice passersby. The Chinese imported ready-made outfits were for men, but there were also some clothes for children. The new outfits were all crisply packed and wrapped, and my father would carefully select the ones to display on hangers and arrange around the store. He had a series of ropes dangling in front of the shop window – these were used to hook hangers and create a vertical display. There was a big wooden table at the front of the store where my dad would set out a few well-placed shirts to show off his current styles and trends. Selling clothes was still a select service based on making personal client connections, and drawing people in. I remember my dad was proud of how he dealt with his customers, and my approach to good customer service took shape under his guidance all those years ago. I learned about buying and selling in his clothes shop. He made a point of knowing his clients' names, he would go out of his way to meet their needs, and he pushed sales by offering clients special discounts if they bought more than one outfit, or if they became regulars.

There was a particular sales banter that shopkeepers used. My father would greet the streams of people passing by, making eye contact with one or two and telling them they were a fine-looking man or woman. He would be holding out a shirt or outfit, saying how good it would look on them. The very fact that the people were in your market lane was already an indication that they were seeking some apparel. The constant engagement with those moving down the lane, my father calling out, "Are you looking for jeans? Do you want a lovely shirt?" – it was the cadence of the business. If a potential client approached, my dad would invite them in and seat them, while he asked about their interests, and preferred designs. Then he would set about industriously selecting a range of items, promoting each one in turn for its style or color or feel of the fabric. Doing the small extra things mattered. If a client said he wanted a blue shirt and my father didn't have the right shade, he would ask the client to hold on while he dashed to other clothes sellers and then returned with an armful of shirts in a variety of blue tones.

My father showed me the psychology of making a sale too. Once the customer was in the store, he would make an elaborate show of opening the packaged outfits, taking them out and using big gestures to show how the shirts would look, pressing the items to the client and letting them touch the fabric. Before the clients even said anything, we would have unwrapped three shirts for them to look at. This personal attention, the disregard for the packaging, making a mess while fussing over the client – it was all a ploy to make them feel almost guilted into buying at least one item after all the effort had been made to open so many possible choices to match their personal needs. My dad would drape the shirt across the men's shoulders, smoothing it out and telling them how nice it looked on them. Then he'd reach for the next shirt to drape, and he'd find some new virtues of how it matched the customer's style. What the clients didn't know was that we had the well-trained skill of being able to carefully repackage each shirt, folded in the precise pristine new way, so they would look untouched for the next customer.

On slow days, some of the market men would gather to play draughts. A few had young boys back at their shops who would act as couriers and run to fetch them when any clients arrived. It was an odd thing, the draught playing, because if you did it during the working day it was seen as a sign of laziness. If you did it in the evenings, it was an acceptable relaxation. But there were no lights in the evening, so it was not really an option to play the games at night. My mother would make the trip to the market to buy fresh produce for lunch, and she would find my dad sitting around with the other market men playing draughts. Even though she never voiced it in front of us, I knew it frustrated her that he was not doing more to manage his business better.

I grew up watching how the business went. There were rumors that my father had once owned a car, a Peugeot, but in my childhood the car was long gone. The clothing business became largely seasonal. People would order outfits for special occasions such as Easter and Christmas. There were hardly any clients stepping into the shop for my dad's attention. Looking back now, I can understand how all that time my father was eating into his business capital, buying goods that did not sell. With fewer clients and more competition, the business began to sink. After a protracted time, my dad's business was virtually gone. Still, he would leave the house every morning, and go to his shop. He relied on friends for what little support he had to buy and sell, and some days, even finding the small money to take transport to the market was hard. By the time I reached secondary school, it was apparent that the business would not recover.

I could see how my dad was struggling, and I watched firsthand as he became more lost and hurt, a grown man brought low by not being able to take care of his own family. I know my father was a good man. He would help around the house, making meals and washing clothes, helping his children get ready for school – never too proud to be a caring family man. But he was a broken man, one without resources to do the things he wanted to do. I saw him bite back words when things were said to him by other men more fortunate. Life humbled him, circumstances incapacitated him. I don't think any man should go through that.

I wonder how my father felt, to know that there was food on the table in our home, and that it came from my mother's efforts. Her garri business was doing well. Unlike clothes, people always needed to buy garri. It was the staple food item that went with the soups that were made each day. The typical family my mother would sell to every day of the week would be households of seven or more people. Father, mother, three or more children, and a relative or two added in under one roof. Interestingly, the garri sales would decrease in holiday periods like Christmas, when families chose to splurge on better meals. But at all other times, there was a good demand for my mother's garri, and as a bonus, she would be able to bring some home so that we would have something to eat at night too.

Cash flow from the garri business was good too. My mother had a book, and she would write down what every family owed her, and she would be consistent with collecting the money. I remember that my parents were building a house back in their home village, and it was my mom who paid for most of it to be done. She would buy all the things we needed daily; she would pay for our school fees and buy our clothes. Yet one of my strongest memories of her was that my mother constantly sacrificed her own needs. I never saw her buy clothes for herself, and she never once entered a restaurant to buy a meal. She placed her personal interests last, and those of her family first.

My mother saved money religiously; it was a ritual that she adhered to regardless of our fortunes – the habit of setting money aside. She did it wisely too. The local women would join in pooling their resources and engage in *akawo*, also called *esusu*, an informal banking system, collecting money daily or weekly. My mother and her friends numbered twelve, and they would do collections every three days. Then, at month end, the women would rotate in taking the savings. My mother always calculated her contributions and rotation so that she would take money in the twelfth month, at the end of the year when our family expenses were higher. That money was always part of a bigger spending plan, where my mother would buy doors or put the roof on the village house. Even as I reflect on my mother's behavior, I can hear my wife's voice telling me now that my own money is always planned away. It was a good habit my mother instilled in me.

My parents had very different businesses. My mother had a low profit margin but high cash flow. My father had good profit margins but very poor cash flow. So, he struggled. When I contrast the way they did business, it has become clear to me that an entrepreneur should seek a business that deals in products or services that are needed by people continuously. Even today, my mother's food business continues to survive because no matter how bad the economy is in Nigeria, people still need to eat. Business should not be dependent on one customer showing up repeatedly, or chasing after customers who have a wide range of options. What happens when that client doesn't come to place an order for a month? What happens when the trend fades? Business should exist without marketing or branding.

Reflecting now, I could see how my father was dying a little on the inside each day. Not making enough sales, not having enough money to bring home to care for his children. It is a terrible life to live. I barely have money on me at any point in time, but I am always only one phone call away from accessing money that I have made or saved. Over the years I have seen the same happen to men in their homes, where a man who has no money speaks, and his family does not listen to him. There is no respect, worst of all, from the children of the house who should listen to their father's guidance. I saw what happened to my dad, and I don't want that in my house, to be a man without resources or the respect of my family. Without the means to do what is important, what needs to be done.

When I was about ten, I was sent to buy something at a nearby house in Borokiri that had a kiosk shop. I saw this old man clutching an empty beer bottle and leaning hard on a walking stick, making his way slowly there to go buy kerosene. I wondered why the old man was doing a task that should have been given to a child in his house. Somehow, I remember telling myself then that I wasn't going to be poor. I was not going to be forced into an old age where I did not have someone who could do the small tasks that no old man should be doing. It was moments like this that added to my impressions of my dad becoming weakened by his failure to make a living for his family, these moments that made me resolve to have a different future.

My mom has a healthy financial way of thinking. She is so good with money. She saves and saves. And she spends wisely. Even now, I never hesitate to give her money because I know she will do one of three things with it. First, she will tithe, and give to her church. Then she will use some of it for one of her plans, most likely buying cement blocks to keep building something somewhere. Last, she will use some of that money to share with the less fortunate. I think I took a lot from her, especially her discipline around money. Every day she would bring in the money she had collected, and she would count it down to the last cent. Just being around her helped me learn the value of being disciplined with money matters. Learning how to count money, learning how to save money, learning how to account for money, learning how to invest, learning how to plan, learning how to be able to take care of children financially. My mother is truly an amazing woman. Today, even though I can say I have helped her buy land and build a house, the truth is that my mother, who is in her sixties, is still contributing and she is still building too.

The choices you make early in life as a man matter. The kind of work you choose to do matters. I would never do a business now where I cannot control my revenue. Managing expenses matters less than having full control over the revenue you can make. I would never do a business that has to be sold through branding and marketing to secure clients. I would rather focus on quality and delivery and an ability to perform consistently well. That's why in the waste management sector, my businesses are always focused on delivering good service consistently well. My clients are my salespeople – it is word of mouth that sells my business because my clients are happy, and their needs are met.

It has served me well to see the relationships that people have with money. My father depended on high margins, but those helped little in a competitive market. Yet, when his business failed it was a friendship that made a difference. When he was at his lowest, sick in body and spirit, someone whom my father knew well gave him a new opportunity to manage an imported clothing store in far-away Abuja. He had to sacrifice and leave his family home, but at least my father could command respect again. Then there was Mr Smith, my Canadian teacher and mentor, who had plenty of money for the pot at home, but he ate it all before the month even ended. His disregard for his finances was almost peculiar, and still he was fervently passionate about the impact he had on enriching the lives of his students with knowledge he served at his table. And finally, there was my mother, her discipline with savings and cents, that carried her far, that fed us and clothed us and schooled us when the family fortunes waned.

People need to be close to others who know how to make and use money. Nowadays, when I see the young men who are eager to buy cars, I look at them and laugh. They are throwing away their futures. If only they could know that it is much better to invest that money instead. I credit the journey that I have taken to both my father and my mother. My mom has taught me discipline with money. With my dad, his customer successes showed me Marketing 101: persuasion beyond any customer resistance. His bigger business failures showed me the importance of being able to stand tall as the man of the house, as one who can take care of the family.

I want to be respected by my wife and children. Love from them is secondary. The way that I show love for them is to work hard, to provide for the family and to put a roof over their head and give them all that they need. This is the pattern: do my normal business, be very efficient with it, be very clever about it, invest any excess money in books, in real estate and in liquid assets. Perhaps that is why I own more houses than pairs of shoes. For me, these are now the basics of growing a business, to be able to care for one's family, and to become financially free.

4
A journey of optimism into my future

My final junior high school year was characterized by a growing sense that as the eldest son, I should be more responsible for taking care of the family, that I too should bear the burden. I could feel it building up, the tension and strain in our home, because each day was a struggle with small money coming in. And in my father's shop, the growing despair as each week the customer numbers went down, and the competition in the market grew. Even though he had almost no sales, when the market closed each night, my dad would have to count his cents or sometimes even borrow from friends to buy bread for us on the way home. There was no hope for the business.

At one time it became clear there was no money for my secondary schooling, so the quiet talk turned to how I should go and serve one of my uncles. The uncle who had once served my dad in his business and who received his start in life because my father had supported him. My dad was torn because he desperately wanted me to continue with my schooling. The uncle had also set a high demand, that I would serve him for a period of seven years, whereafter he would settle me by giving me money to start up my own life. So, it came that I left school, barely out of my childhood, to go work for my uncle. Yet my parents resolve that their eldest son should be properly educated prevailed. Soon I stopped, and magically – because I do not know where or how they found the money – I returned to the classroom for my secondary schooling.

Perhaps this also spurred my hunger for education and led to me arriving at Mr Smith's doorstep. It seemed as if all was well again. One of my father's oldest friends was a clothes importer. He had set up a shop in Abuja, the city that had become the capital of Nigeria in the 1990s. Abuja was in the center of Nigeria, some four hundred miles from Port Harcourt, and about a ten-hour drive by rough road. This friend of my father was importing European menswear, and with Abuja being the political center, it was a good place for a store with fine clothing. The friend had heard of my father's misfortune, because by now my dad's business had almost closed. There was very little stock on his shelves and other than having an occasional customer in need of a shirt, my father was home most of the time, ailing and weak. This good friend offered my father the opportunity to manage the Abuja store, and there was relief in our home that my father would be earning good money again.

Suddenly, my dad was back in business, his health restored, eyes bright, and his skin glowing. The first time he returned from Abuja for a family visit, he brought us all many things. I especially remember that he brought my mother some new dresses, and that he took me aside and said how happy he was that I was staying in school. He said he had big plans to build again, to fix our house. There was this renewed hope and enthusiasm in the home, and we were glad for it. I focused on my schoolwork, returning to live and study with Mr Smith and the boys, day after day tackling the math problems that he set for me and feeling positive about the future.

I clearly remember the day I was deeply engaged in my books at Smith's house when the message came that it was very important, I should return home immediately. When I got to our house, everything was eerily quiet. My sister came to me, she said she needed to tell me something, and that I should not cry. Then she told me they said our dad has passed on. What? Why now, I thought. How did it happen that now, when my father had found his feet again in Abuja, that he should die? Why did he not die when he was sick, and the business was gone. It made no sense to me that my father who had been happy and bright on his journeys to and from Abuja could suddenly be dead. He had even bought cement blocks and some new steel gates and was coming to start on the building he had promised.

It was a shock. Here I was at eighteen, and my father was unexpectedly dead. What had happened, I kept wondering as our household was thrust into mourning. People started coming to the house to express their condolences. I could see the extended pity in their eyes. It wasn't just that my dad died, it was the fact that the house we were staying in was in a poor condition. The roof had rusted through and by the time the landlord had been persuaded to fix it, the ceiling had been ruined, it was leaking and had big holes in it, which the landlord had refused to repair. It was a mess, and we had simply been growing up in this state of disrepair. Now there was no place to hide our hardship and I felt ashamed for the first time. I was embarrassed that everybody could visit and see where and how we were living in abject poverty. It was a time where I was forced to raise my head up high, even though inside I felt the ravages of being poor.

There again, something in my youthful thoughts said that it was not my house. It was my father, my mother, their livelihoods, and mixed fortunes, that had brought us to this place of scarcity and ruin. Yet I could not escape the reality that as children, our lives were shaped by my parents' fortunes too. Whether growing up rich or poor, as a child you are affected by what happens in your house under your parents' decisions. After my dad died – we later heard it was a liver condition, likely hepatitis – I started to return home more regularly. I was still schooling with Smith, but I became more aware of my mother's efforts to keep the family going. She was now our primary provider, a widow with five children.

My mom had started selling eggs, in addition to her garri business. There was a woman trader who was bringing in thousands of crates of eggs in a large truck, coming from one of the neighboring states. This Yoruba trader would sell to all the shops, and my mom had arranged to take ten crates from her each week. You could tell that the trader did not regard my mom as an important client because she had such a small order. But that small order required logistics to distribute. I told my mother I would help with her egg business, because she needed someone to carry individual crates to her handful of clients, wherever they were located.

I started walking from shop to shop, asking store owners if they wanted to buy cartons of eggs. I went to shop owners who previously had to go to the market to buy crates of eggs, knowing they would be paying the cost of taxi fare for transport. My goal was to create more convenience for them. I also came on the idea that I would offer them credit, so that they could pay me only once the eggs were sold. It struck me that these clients would lose money if the crates they transported from the market contained any cracked eggs. And so, I made a further deal with them, to replace any cracked eggs in the crates I sold for free. It was not too long before virtually all the shops in the area were buying their egg crates from me. Our growth was organic, and almost every week we would add to the number of crates we were taking from the Yoruba trader.

I grew my mother's egg business to a maximum of one thousand crates in a week, but on average over time, we consistently delivered several hundred crates to our client shopkeepers each week. From a business standpoint, it was interesting for me to learn more about logistics, as well as supply and demand. Getting egg crates, removing cracked ones, selling those we could salvage at a cheaper price to food sellers who were frying them, so that we reduced waste. Distributing the good crates to all our customers, keeping track of their orders and payments, managing the flow of the core business. Just by focusing on that core business, we were guaranteed to succeed. I believe that applies to whatever business you are in. Sometimes I see people lose focus on what is important for their businesses to succeed. They get distracted by talking up a brand and creating an active social media presence to build followers. Yet they fail to keep their customers happy in the day-to-day interactions of their business.

I rarely lost any of my customers in the egg trade business. If you are consistently doing what your customer needs and values, your business will grow. The customer will recommend you to other customers. In those times when your egg shipments are delayed, the customers will be loyal to you, willing to wait instead of going off to the market to buy their stock. Just by focusing on what was valuable to my customers, we were steadily growing my mother's egg business. The family was doing well, and as my schooling year was also nearing completion, we had the good news that I had been accepted to study mechanical engineering at a polytechnic college.

Personally, my interests in life were shifting. At eighteen, I was actively involved in Scripture Union, and I had met some young men – Kodjo and Francis – who had big plans for their future. Kodjo had heard from his cousin Dr Kofi that there were opportunities in Ghana in the oil industry. My head started to turn to the anticipation of leaving Nigeria for some big adventure. At this time my elder sister had taken ill, and my mother had gone to take care of her. The egg business was flourishing; we had perfected the supply and credit process and had a good customer base. But as a young man, somewhere inside me there was an unexpressed feeling that if I could only leave Nigeria, then I would leave all our problems and poverty behind. I listened keenly to Kodjo and Francis as they made plans to go, and we started talking about how I would accompany them.

Dr Kofi – Doc – was the one who had ties to the energy ministry and who filled our heads with this story of land in Ghana and the promise of an oil deal. Doc had big plans for me too. His wife was living in Austria, and he told me that I could go abroad to complete my studies, and that he and his wife would help make that happen. Soon we were gathering all our papers to apply for travel documents. My mother was still at my sick sister's bedside when I went to tell her of my decision to leave Nigeria. I could see in her eyes that she wanted me to stay, even as she gave me her blessing and said I could go. She knew I was young, and she did not want to hold me back. Of course, I was a young African, and all young Africans somehow believe their lives will be better and their fortunes greater if they go to the US, or Europe. For me, the promise of studying in Austria was a big lure.

The journeys that we young Africans take are journeys of optimism! The preparation took several months. I clearly recall one time, Francis and I had to accompany Doc to Lagos to get some travel plans sorted. All the while, Doc had been reassuring us that our passports were at the embassy waiting for the visa paperwork to be completed. Yet, at the hotel in Lagos, on a day that Doc left us to go into the city, Francis decided to look around. When he opened a drawer, there were our passports, the visa application papers untouched. Even though Doc was revealing his lack of credible character, our eyes did not want to see the truth. Because then we would jeopardize our one big opportunity. So, we made excuses in our heads, thinking there must be a good reason, and we kept our mouths shut, waiting for the next step.

Eventually, the long-promised journey came. Coming from Lagos the first time, when we got to the Ghana border, that drive was one of the most significant experiences in my life. You must understand that in Nigeria, we lived without electricity – only the wealthy could afford to buy and run generators that powered houses and buildings. The journey by road took us through the narrow sliver countries of Benin, then Togo – crossing our first border post at Cotonou, then again at Lome, driving around three hundred miles. As we crossed the final border post in the dark and made our way past villages and towns in Ghana, the thing that struck me most was that they all had lights. I was taken aback, because I had never seen lights everywhere, and it was like that all the way to Accra. In Nigeria, electricity was a miracle. In Ghana, it seemed an ordinary occurrence. We reached our destination, a house in the suburb of Osu in Accra, the capital city of Ghana. I remember coming out the next night again just to look at the houses and buildings around us to see that there was indeed light. It was marvelous, and my future certainly felt like it was bright.

5
A million Ghana Cedis means nothing

In my first few days in Ghana, I was to experience a few more surprises, beyond the delight of having electricity available almost all the time. One morning I went down to the open-air market, wanting to buy oranges. The food sellers had stalls piled up with some new and other familiar foodstuffs, and in a few places, there were children selling loose oranges. I listened as they called out, "One million cedis." Thinking I had misheard, I approached one of the boys who held up an orange and said, "1.2 million." I had only ever traded in Nigerian naira, and it took me a short while to realize that the Ghana cedi was much weaker as a currency. Back in Lagos, you couldn't even imagine what a million naira looked like. Yet here in Ghana, people brandished these cedi currency notes printed with million values.

The house in Osu Ako Adjei where we stayed was on a compound with four other houses. Like many properties in Ghana, the land was the subject of a lengthy legal dispute. Ghana's tribal land tenure system and land title practices have long been the source of unending litigation; compounded by shoddy land surveys and boundary disputes, as well as double sales and all forms of maladministration. When the compound landowner had passed away some years before, his children – who occupied two houses on the land – had demanded that others living on the land should start paying them rent. Kodjo's father was one of those refusing to pay; he had built a house right at the back of the lot, and it was a good-sized space, with three small bedrooms, a toilet, and a kitchen. He disputed the rent claims and would not give up the property. That's how Kodjo's brother Evans came to stay in the house, to occupy it while the court case continued.

It was here that Kodjo brought us when we came from Nigeria, and where his brother Evans agreed we could stay. Each of our rooms had a single naked bulb dangling from a wire – not pretty, but still a useful source of light for someone not used to having electricity at the flick of a switch. The compound itself and houses in it were unkempt – nothing was painted, the grass around was wild with more weeds than lawn, and there was scrap littering the shared yard. In one corner, there was an old used car that was just a rusted heap of metal. Still, the disputed house was a place to eat and sleep as we tried to make our plans materialize into some form of income.

The discoveries during the first days in Ghana were beautiful in a way, even though there was a lot of uncertainty. Early on, our presence created some excitement around the compound, especially with all the talk of lucrative oil deals. Ghana's oil discoveries were recent, while Nigeria had been wheeling and dealing in this black gold for years. Our investment talks about setting up an oil refinery had sparked some success as Doc and Kodjo engaged with Prof. Aaron Mike Ocquaye, who was Ghana's Minister for Energy. There were those around us who were eager to offer support, changing our naira to cedis, inviting us to share their Ghanaian food – all for the promise of a grand investment deal. Times were still good. Over Christmas, I went all by myself to Vani in the Volta region, and I did a mountain hike, giving me time to truly enjoy the scenery. Gradually though, talks with investors stalled and the deal seemed further and further away.

In time, we were all waiting to hear the outcome of the court case and we moved about the compound essentially as unwanted guests. Each morning I would wake, not sure if this was the day that I was going to be sacked from the house following a court order. Also treading carefully around Kodjo's brother, Evans, who stayed there first, and who was the reason we had been allowed into the house at all. He was getting increasingly more frustrated with our presence there and his moods would shift from being generous to treating us poorly, insisting that we serve him and clean up after him. Meals were contentious – I didn't have much money and could seldom afford to buy food. Evans would finish eating and give his bowl to me with meagre leftovers – and I would wash the bowl knowing that's the only food I would have to eat.

"Keep yourself going," that was what I kept telling myself. I didn't see it as suffering because the optimism and the chance to be in this different part of the world, these feelings kept me positive even when day to day life was hard. There was the glimmer of hope of a deal, if Doc could find a way to leverage the energy ministry connections he still had. So what if Evans did not want us in the house because we were affecting his life. True, his girlfriend could no longer come around because his brother and his brother's friends were now underfoot. But we had come to

Ghana with a purpose. Francis was also with us, and his wife was there too. Then she became pregnant, and suddenly it added to the fullness of all of us in this small, disputed house in an Osu compound. The house was getting crowded and there was no privacy, and few prospects.

I learned that if your dreams are big enough, then your problems will shrink in the face of them. I was focused on one thing only; the promise Doc had made that his wife would help me go to Austria to study engineering. While everything negative was happening around me, it did not matter. I saw it all as being temporary and believed life would get better. I remember not being able to tell my mother about how difficult my new circumstances were. Africans who travel, when they get caught up in dire situations so much so that they cannot even go home – they least of all can tell the families they left behind the truth of their plight. They cannot appear to have failed, and so they say nothing of the hard times to their loved ones. There would be calls, and I would say all is fine, I am doing well. When my mother and I spoke, I would marvel about the power that was always on, as if all my problems were somehow solved by the constant light.

With time it was becoming clear that Doc and his promises of oil deals and studies abroad were going nowhere. Doc eventually abandoned us, leaving me to stay with Kodjo and his brother Evans, and Francis and the wife and the newborn baby. Nobody knew where Doc had gone, and he had taken my dreams of schooling in Austria with him. Our new struggle became finding ways to make it through each day. I went to work for Kodjo's father. What really happened was that Kodjo's father, Mr Odjor, had a well-established pest control business called Sunrise

International, and I would go hang out in the hopes he would hire me for any task for the day. The company had a good footing, with government contracts that reportedly included some sort of joint Cuban venture. When I was lucky, there would be three or four household fumigation jobs per week. It was strictly no job, no pay. At least the small money I would make for a day's work with Sunrise International would be enough to buy whatever food portion I could afford to take back to the house to cook for the others.

Kodjo was more creative. He had kept all the documents that Doc had put together, papers that showed connections to the Energy Ministry and potential land deals with opportunities in Ghana's now burgeoning oil sector. Kodjo would show these documents to various people and get them to invest money in the oil project. Fronting him the money while he worked on the details of this supposed oil deal that I knew was in the empty promises pipeline. Francis helped him. So, there was some money coming in from Kodjo's pitches for funding, and my small bits of work if Kodjo's father had a job for me. There were days I would just sit at home, watch television, having nothing to do and feeling endlessly miserable. And there was rising tension because Francis felt the money was being distributed unfairly, and that as a family man with a wife and child, he deserved a bigger share. It didn't make sense to me. All we were doing was trying to manage with hand-to-mouth earnings. Nothing was fair, it was all a struggle to survive.

I became so skinny. I recently showed my wife a photo of how I looked back then, tall, and so thin, with sunken features. Those days the ladies never talked to me and looking at that picture it was easy to understand why. It was obvious that I was not getting much to eat, and even emotionally, I was living in a house that resembled a war zone of ill feelings, and a compound where the threat of the court case outcome hung heavily over our heads. I had to find my peace in there and keep going.

There was one man who became instrumental in how I made it through the hardest of days, time and again. Pastor Seth Odonkor and his wife had a small kiosk near where we lived; they sold tinned goods with the kind of stuff people needed to make staple Ghanaian meals – garlic, onion, peppers. We met one day when I went to buy tinned tomatoes; we began talking, and as time passed and the money to buy at his kiosk became scarce, I would still go sit with him. He would teach the word of the Lord, and we would discuss the views he shared. I think he knew I was not that much interested in the Lord's word. I was hungry for food, not religion. Pastor Seth's wife made it clear she did not appreciate my presence at their kiosk; she would leave for the market whenever I arrived. But Pastor Seth would wait for her to go, and he would preach a little, and then he would bring me a banana. That banana was the best accompaniment to the word of the Lord.

Today, Pastor Seth is on my payroll. I support him because I will never forget how he got me through the most difficult times when I came to Ghana. I speak to him once a month. Back then, he was the one person I could go to, just to talk. I seldom told him of my circumstances; instead, I engaged with him around the Bible. The Bible and the bananas helped more than he could know. There were days that I would be walking across the compound of the house where we were perching – which is what they say in Ghana when you are a temporary guest. The owner of the Osu house would see me, and his resentment was etched on his face. I was not paying rent and he wanted me to go. I would greet him, and he would not see any need to talk to me. He was angry, and it showed.

Just recently I went into a restaurant and saw one of the landowner's children who had pushed for our eviction – he was the chef there, but he did not know that I recognized him from all those years ago. He came out of the kitchen, greeted me as "Sir" and asked what I wanted to eat, enquiring avidly after my health. I wondered had he known I was the one he and his siblings had sacked from their late father's property in Osu Ako Adjei 20 years before, if he would even have stepped out of the kitchen to serve me. I was that young skinny Nigerian man who had lived on that same compound where he was growing up. He too had been a small boy who must have seen how we were sacked. Eventually the children had obtained their court order, and we were told we had to leave. When we got the order, I felt most sorry for Francis and his wife and their little baby boy. Sometimes the world can be a cold place where nobody cares about anybody. Did that owner ever stop to wonder when he ordered that eviction, where that baby boy would sleep?

On the day we were asked to leave, when the court order was given, that evening I went to meet with my friend, Pastor Seth. As I returned later to the Osu house, I saw a taxi driving away. Kodjo and Francis and his wife were in it, and they were going without saying anything to me. They just left. Evans was still there at the house. We went to bed and at dawn, while we were still sleeping, suddenly we heard the banging and smashing of wooden batons as we were roused from our beds and chased out of the house. I had to grab my clothes and go. Evans and I walked the streets of Osu for a while. At a point, he called his brother Kodjo and asked him where they were and where I was. I listened as Kodjo told his brother he should not worry about me, that they had left me sleeping in my room and that I was fine. We were standing at a T-junction; it was late, and dark. Evans looked at me and told me from now on I was on my own. I clasped my belongings to me, feeling the weight of loneliness in a strange country as Evans went his way.

I recently took a friend to show him that junction and told him that this was the junction to nowhere. That night, after I had watched my friends drive away and leave me behind, and watched Evans turn his back and go too, I realized that I was at a crossroads and had no idea whether to go left or go right, or if I should go back in the other direction. For some reason, I turned towards the ocean direction and started walking.

That first night of being homeless, I found a place on the beach under some palm trees, among fallen fronds and coconuts. It was a long night, the ocean air was cold, and there was a strong wind blowing. I found a coconut tree trunk to lay on, and pulled some leaves and branches, trying to fashion a place I could rest, but it was so difficult to find any sleep. Later in the night, I heard a growing murmuring and watched as a group of people clothed in white and carrying lanterns appeared to start some sort of rituals on the shore. Afraid, I grabbed my stuff and crept away into the night. Soon I came across a bunch of rasta men, sleeping rough on the beach – one of them stirred and saw me. He said I looked odd carrying this small bag of possessions, and he questioned what I was doing. I said I needed a place to sleep. He replied that he would go and ask if I could stay, but as soon as he disappeared into the dark, I ran away again.

I ended up sleeping by the roadside, on hard concrete, next to an open gutter, with my head on a piece of PVC piping. In the morning I made my way to a public restroom to wash and dress. I'm not sure those places still exist today, but I thank God for that washroom facility back then. I cleaned myself up and went to Kodjo's father's house, praying I would still find some kindness there for the odd job or two. With hindsight, I am grateful that we were evicted, sacked, chased from that Osu house. Living there was turning me into a beggar. The dreams and plans we had when we came to Ghana were gone. It was foolish to keep clinging to them. I was on my own, and I needed to count on myself to find a solution for the way forward.

6

Homeless and hungry become my constant companions

Being homeless is so much more than not having a roof over your head. I already knew about poverty and living hand to mouth. Now I would discover that all humans have another survival state, one where they need shelter and security. After we were turned out of the Osu compound, my life changed in ways I could not have imagined when I dreamed the big optimistic dream. Being homeless meant that each night I faced the problem of where I would sleep. It meant that I had to carry my whole life with me, my few clothes and books and parts of who I was that I had brought from Nigeria, and it all fit into a small, dilapidated bag that had once been the hope of a grand adventure.

For a time, I would make my way first to a mechanic's shop as darkness fell. People would sometimes leave their vehicles overnight when they were being repaired, and some cars in the mechanic's work yard had simply been abandoned. Such cars made good sleeping places – but most of the time they were all occupied. The owner of the mechanic shop had mates, and the young boys working for him, and they would also be bedding down in the cars. You would have to scrounge about for an unlocked door and an empty car seat to lay your head. Sleeping in strangers' cars, with the smell of grease and motor oil – that counted for a good night.

On nights when I could not find an open car, I would move about the streets and compounds, dodging dogs, and clambering in bushes, until I found an absent homeowner's porch or perhaps a balcony that offered some shelter. In the mornings, every day I would rise and make my way back to Kodjo's father's business, praying he would give me a job. If I had been earning in dollars those days, $1 would have been able to buy me a small bag of oranges. The money I made when I was working was a lot less than a dollar – more the equivalent of two Ghana cedis today. On days I had work, I would be paid just enough to buy two small portions of *koko*, which is made of corn dough and hot water, sweetened with sugar. Day in and day out that was my only source of sustenance when I first came to be homeless.

My friend Pastor Seth had an arrangement with a school, where he would hold his church services on Sunday in one of their classrooms. When he became aware that I was sleeping rough on the streets, Pastor Seth took the key he had to the classroom and duplicated it. And for almost a year, that classroom became my place of abode, the closest thing I had to a permanent residence. It was not a home – how could it be when the only access I had was under cover of darkness after all the teachers and school children had left for the day, and when I had to rise very early to make sure I could sneak away without being discovered? At night, I would take the student desks and pack them in a formation of four to six, then lie on top of them to sleep. It was almost impossible to rest, because the wooden desks were sloped at an angle, and I would lie so that I could balance my weight. If I wasn't bent in a certain way, I would slip off the table surfaces once I had fallen asleep. But slanted tables were better than cold cement. Then, each morning before the students arrived, I would pack all my belongings in my bag and head out.

I got creative after a while. Somewhere I came across a very big box, it had once had a deep freeze chest inside it – and I dragged it back to the school. I put it on the ground and for the first time I could sleep straight, and it was almost a good night's sleep. But close to the ground there were many more mosquitoes, an inevitable way to get malaria. I partially solved the mosquito problem by buying cheap insecticide coils that I could light, and they would burn slowly at night. But on some nights when the wind was strong, the mosquito coils would die out and soon in my sleep the mosquitoes would be feasting on my blood. I used to joke that I didn't think I would ever have malaria again because all the mosquito bites I endured made that the malaria parasites could not tell the difference between my blood and the mosquito.

As I mentioned, the school classroom was also where we had our church services on Sunday, yet none of the church members aside from Pastor Seth knew that I was sleeping there at night. In the same way that when my mother asked, I would assure her all is well, with my fellow churchgoers I would never complain about my hardship. I'm not sure why it was like that. I have forgotten whether in those conversations, I simply avoided any personal details, or if somehow, I never expected that the solution to my problems would be found beyond what I could do. And so, I kept doing. Every day I got up and walked to Kodjo's father, and if there was work I would do it diligently, regardless of pains in my body or hunger pangs.

Consciously I had made a pact with myself to save money, half of anything that I earned. More and more often I would wake in the middle of the night and feel extreme hunger, and I realized I would have to better manage how and when to eat my small food portions. The *koko* mixture was not sustaining enough on its own, and this led me to start buying a piece of bread or two. I could not afford bread that had margarine on it – instead I bought my own small tub of cheap margarine with a bottle of groundnut paste, which Americans call peanut butter. These I carried with me in my backpack for when I could buy a slice of bread. Still, I would stick to the meal plan of eating only twice a day, just rotating my food choices between early morning and late night. On some days if we had worked hard, I would eat my second meal by the afternoon. Those days were more difficult, because I knew as I was eating that food, I would endure hunger in the night.

All the while, I was busy saving money. There were a few occasions when I would reach a point of being so hungry that I would buy kenkey. This is a mix of fermented white corn that is boiled and wrapped in a maize husk. It is normally served with a peppery soup – a hot blend of spicy chilies – and a piece of fish. All I could afford was a little bit of the peppery sauce; I would never buy fish with it. I would get some water to wash it down. Other times I would get some fufu, which is cassava that has been pounded into a starchy, smooth, and slightly sour dough ball. It is normally eaten with light goat soup or a meat stew, and you pinch off a piece from the dough and roll it in your fingers, then dip it into the soup or stew. Except I never had enough money for soup or stew. It was rare to see someone buying fufu or kenkey without fish or meat. It became a source of amusement for my fellow workers.

Occasionally, Kodjo's father would treat his workers to a meal on days when the client had paid well or offered a bonus tip. He would even buy drink for us, and we would all regard that as a good day. But when he would give us money to buy food, I would try not to eat my portion. I would pack it away and only consume my normal miserly meal. I continued that way for the longest time, living in the school secretly, controlling whatever food I could afford, and saving, saving, saving.

After a period, two more church members became aware of my homeless plight. Forlonshor, who was caretaking a house for some people who lived abroad in America; and Ocansey, who had a room in his family home that he sometimes shared with his sisters, and if they were not there, he would occasionally make space for me to stay over. I arranged with Forlonshor to leave my clothes and few possessions at his house. With Ocansey the agreement was more informal. I would arrive at his home and wait for him, and if I was lucky, I would get a plate of food, and if I was luckier still, his sisters would leave, and I would bed down in his room for that night. On nights when he could only offer a meal, then he would walk me back to the school once we had eaten. Forlonshor was less free to invite me around; he had to be careful that the homeowners would not find out he had guests because that would jeopardize his caretaking job.

My homelessness took on a new cycle of sleeping in various places, none of which were readily accessible. The school was becoming a more difficult location to stay in secret. It was quite a distance to walk from Osu to the Ring Road, under the beating sun or in the pouring rain, to the place where I would be working. It is hard to admit it, but there were times when I wished a car would knock me down so that I could be taken up in hospital and be in a coma, and I prayed it would be a rich man whose car would strike me so that all my problems would be over. Thank God that never happened. Life continued, without any stability or consistency. I didn't know it then, but somehow, I believed it would be better.

Sometimes there would be no work for days on end. Knowing that work was scarce, my savings habit became even more brutal and focused – I would never allow myself to spend more than half of any money I earned. Still, there were highlights. Friday nights and Saturday mornings were my best times while I was sleeping in the classroom. The whole school would become quiet at the end of the week, and I would be able to sleep late on a Saturday. I would take my time getting up, happy there was no rush. I felt a free man; I would read, I would sleep, I would use my small radio and listen to music – it was a time I would relish. But there were other times when my secret life would be unexpectedly disrupted. I remember one time we had worked hard, and I overslept. And there was this young schoolgirl who came to class very early in the morning, sometimes by 5 am. This particular day when I overslept, luckily I heard her opening another classroom door, and I scrambled frantically to grab my stuff and narrowly managed to disappear through a second door before she discovered me. It was funny to think my life could be chased up by a child, that such a thing would scare me.

There were other challenges I encountered while staying on the school property. The school children who were tasked with locking the building would get padlocks mixed up and I would end up without a key that fitted the lock to the church classroom. I would have to wait until the weekend again when the school master would give Pastor Seth a new key, and I would have to duplicate that one. Once when that happened, it was raining heavily, and I could not go anywhere. I found the most sheltered place at the school, on a veranda, in a corridor area, and lay down. At a point I heard noises and felt someone coming to lie by me. It was a mad man from the area, one of the neglected mentally ill people who roamed the streets of Osu. He stank of sweat and urine and filth and oblivious desperation. We got through the night, lying against each other, the water droplets falling against my skin, both of us soaked and shivering against the wind.

It wasn't safe to sleep out in the open, so on nights that I would be locked out of the school, I would still seek shelter off the streets. I would walk down the nearby roads, looking for a gate that was unlocked. On such a night I found a gate open to a complex, and I made myself comfortable just inside the portal. One of the tenants arrived back late that night and declared how happy he was to see that the landlord had finally listened to their requests to get a security man, so they could keep the riffraff out. I am sure he saw my work coveralls and made that assumption, and I kept quiet, not saying anything. But I decided to stay awake for a while longer until I was sure no more people would be coming in, and

I moved my things to a corridor and settled for the night, getting up early to leave by 5 am again.

Life was hard, and I no longer had any clear plan in mind. I went day by day. If homelessness and hunger were my companions, they kept company with my books and the inspiration I drew from the words of *Richest Man in Babylon* and *Think and Grow Rich*. Sacrifice and saving – that was how I was building a future, even if I had no idea how that future looked from the streets where I was living. I managed to juggle sleeping spaces and hustle every day until I was able to save up enough money. It took me over a year to save the sum of 60 Ghana cedis. In my opinion, it was that 60 cedis that became the start of my real life. Sixty Ghana cedis gave me options.

I will never know where I found the strength to set those cedis aside even when my belly was burning and churning with gnawing pangs. I just know that one day I woke up and counted my savings and saw that I had a whole sixty Ghana cedis. Sixty Ghana cedis.

7
Choosing a path for my future

There are moments in your life when an option is placed before you, and the paths you can see lead in uncertain directions. With 60 Ghana cedis in my pocket, the choice seemed much clearer. I had found out that if I went down to the bus station that day, I could buy a bus ticket that would take me from Accra to Lagos, and it would cost me exactly 60 cedis. Lagos, Nigeria – home, family, a future that seemed to offer a steady path. After all, I had once before raised my mother's business, and our family fortunes had grown profitable. Decision made, I gathered my belongings from Forlonshor's place, packed all my stuff in my bag, and started walking towards the Accra bus depot.

At some point I passed the Osu compound where Kodjo, Francis, and I had lived with Evans when we first came to Ghana. It stirred memories, not of regret, but of dreams dashed. All I wanted was to keep moving, towards that bus that would take me home to Nigeria. I kept walking until I was at a junction, and I needed to choose where to turn to make my way to town. Suddenly I heard it, as loud as a voice speaking directly in my ear, crystal clear and insistent in its tone.

"Do you know this sixty cedis can change your life?"

I stopped in my tracks. My mind started spinning. The thoughts came, the knowledge I had gained from working for Kodjo's father, the expertise around chemicals that were needed for fumigation, all I had learned almost unconsciously on the job, day to day. Now, without hesitation I turned in the direction of town where I knew I would find the Agrimat store at Madina. It was a big store that had all sorts of agricultural equipment and supplies, including pesticides and insecticides. I walked determinedly until I got there and took the bus ticket money out my pocket to buy a fumigation knapsack with some chemicals. Leaving the store, my second thought was how I would market my fumigation services, and I recalled with the egg business I had gone from shop owner to shop owner. Ocansey came to mind; he had a laptop at his house, and I rushed back to him, and we worked to design a pamphlet.

I was driven by gut instinct, determined that those 60 cedis were going to change my life. As for the early advertising, I am pretty sure my pamphlet had spelling errors in it, but it was something tangible to hand out to the customers I was starting to see in my mind's eye. I designed the leaflet in a way that we could use an A4 sheet of paper and print four per sheet. Ocansey was able to get access to a printer where he worked, at a Lebanese shopping mall called Melcom. He printed the pamphlets, and I began the process of distributing them. In those days there were no street postal boxes – in fact, most streets were not even named. Every day that I wasn't working with Kodjo's father at Sunrise International, I would go about from house to house, compound to compound, shop to shop. If the owner was there, I would press a flyer in their hand. Sometimes I would be bold enough to enter a yard and go knock on doors if I thought the homeowner was in the house. If I only encountered a security guard, I would make small talk and then leave my pamphlet with them. Where gates were locked, I would find a crack or a gap, and tuck my leaflet in a way it would be found.

By this time, I had been away from Nigeria for many months, and my personal wardrobe had dwindled down to a shirt, a pair of trousers, and brown sandals. I washed the clothes almost every day. But the sandals took the most wear and tear, with all my random trekking to drop off flyers on the days I wasn't working for Kodjo's father. Soon those sandals had developed big holes in them and seen many variations of repairs so that I could keep on walking. And then it happened, I got my very first client. It was such a small job, to do fumigation and be paid the equivalent of three cedis, which was slightly more than Kodjo's father was paying me. It gave me hope, making me believe that my dreams could still come true. I continued with the same cycle until I got the second job from a shop located on the first floor, above the well-known bookstore called Anointed Books. The shop had an attractive display that consisted of flowerpots arranged outside a window front, and it was my good fortune that the plants had attracted many ants.

This time I was paid the equivalent of six cedis. I calculated that if I could keep reducing the amount of time between the small fumigation contracts that I was getting, I would be able to grow my earnings much faster than if I continued working for Kodjo's father. My big break came with the third job. The client was a young Nigerian man who was employed by one of the telecommunication companies, and who was living in the well-to-do suburb of Cantonments. He drove a Mercedes E-Class, and one day he drove past me on the street and saw my fumigation backpack. He opened his car window and asked if I would be able to come spray at his house. He described the house, and I realized it was quite big, so when he asked for a price, I said what amounted to 250 cedis. He agreed without hesitation, and that was when I realized my small backpack sprayer was not going to be up to the task.

I turned to my good friend Pastor Seth and asked if he would loan me money to buy a bigger, better motorized fumigation machine – and I promised to repay him as soon as the job was complete. Pastor Seth loaned me the money; I bought the machine, did the job, got paid in full plus an extra tip, and was then able to repay Pastor Seth. Ocansey offered to let me keep the fumigation machine at his place for safekeeping, especially as I was still drifting to find a place to lay my head at night. Inside me, something had shifted, and I knew that it would be foolish to continue working for Kodjo's father. With just three jobs I had earned more money in a short space of time than all those long hard months it took for me to save 60 cedis. So, I stopped going to Sunrise International to pick occasional jobs from Mr Odjor and began seriously seeking my own clients instead.

The books I had been reading had inspired me to consider creating multiple streams of income, and perhaps personal hardship had also given me the drive to make money wherever I could. It was just a question of how to make it happen. Serendipity! That's how many business ventures emerge. One of my early fumigation contracts was with Tullow Oil – a British company that had recently set up in Ghana. I was talking with the manager one day and he asked if I could do waste management. His problem was that there was no reliable refuse collection service for his personal home in Cantonment. He offered me the sum of 60 cedis per month. I announced I could do it, even though I had no experience collecting waste. It suddenly opened my eyes to the size of the problem – everywhere I went, households were burdened with piles of uncollected trash.

Of course, I never had the resources to do the job at first, and so I teamed up with a coconut seller who had a hand-drawn flatbed trailer on four wheels. He did the refuse collection work for two weeks and then stopped without informing me. When I found out and asked why, he said the distance from Osu to Cantonment was too far. That meant I started a process of finding a network of young men who had handcarts much closer to where we had our work, and I began to do the collection with them to make sure the job got done. I also gained more clients in the wealthy Cantonment area simply by looking for households where the trash was piled up, and asking if they were interested in a reliable collection service. Soon, I had two income streams.

As the fumigation and waste management work started increasing, I turned to one of the men who attended church with me, named Bismarck, to see if he could help me out. I should tell you a bit more about our church – as you remember, it was held in a classroom, so we were a small group under Pastor Seth. The church followed the teachings of William M. Branham, a self-styled Elijah prophet with a mix of faith healing and doomsday messages – although I am not sure any of us knew of his racist leanings towards the Ku Klux Klan. I remember certain strict beliefs, such as that women had to keep their natural hair and not wear wigs. Men like Bismarck would firmly grasp my hand after the service, and ask "Brother, how are you?" Bismarck himself had no idea that I was still homeless and sleeping in the church at night. And even if he had known, I am sure he would still have helped me, because that is his nature. He was a few years older than me and had little education – but he had a good heart and a willing work ethic.

One thing about Bismarck: he dressed very well on Sundays, but during the week he looked disheveled because he was also taking whatever odd jobs he could find. Cutting down trees and clearing land, packing fruit for a vendor in the morning and evening. And saying yes to helping me. I paid him as we got work, for each job, but could not offer him anything permanent. Bismarck's own accommodation was scant – he and two of his daughters were sleeping rough in an uncompleted building. There were prostitutes who slept in the same building, and it was a bad living arrangement. Even though I was still homeless, I helped Bismarck and his daughters to find a better place, a small compound house. At least I could go sit with them some evenings and enjoy the spoiled fruit he brought back from the old ladies he helped with their stall.

It was good because Bismarck and I worked well together. One evening we got to the Tullow residence where we collected trash, and the security man opened the gate for us. Typically, the bins were heavy, and required some effort to drag them from the back, where they were standing next to the compound's electric fence. This night, I was between the bins and the fence when I pulled at one of them – only to lose my balance because the bin was empty. The moment I hit the electric fence I felt an intense jolt and I lost consciousness. When I came round, Bismarck recounted how he was lucky enough to be wearing rubber gloves and had been able to pull me off the fence! I told him we needed to hurry to get to the next client, and it was only when we were walking that I realized I had a bitter burnt taste in my mouth. I was lucky God spared my life that night.

There was much I had to learn about doing business, and in those days, I was extremely naïve. I will never forget a certain incident with a client. Up until that point, all our business was done with cash transactions. One day a client asked if I would accept a check because he did not have money on him. I said yes, and when he asked for my company's name, I said the first thing that came to mind: JNRS Pest Control Ltd. It sounded right, and the acronym was based on four phrases I heard often in church. Jehovah Jireh, God will provide. Jehovah Nissi, the Lord is my banner. Jehovah Rapha, the Lord is our healer. And Jehovah Shalom, the Lord is peace. Jireh Nissi Rapha Shalom.

The client printed the name neatly on the check. JNRS Ltd. Looking at the check, I realized I would need to go to a bank with it. It occurred to me that the bank would probably want proof that I worked for a company called JNRS, so I went to my friend Ocansey and asked him to make up an employee badge for me with my name on it, a fake employee number, and a sort of company logo. I laugh now at the simplicity of my thinking, even the wishfulness of it all. The next day I walked into the bank to cash the check, and the bank teller pushed it and my so-called employee ID back over the counter to me. She told me to go ask my boss where the company had its bank account because I would first have to pay the check into the company account before I could cash it. I left the bank looking at that piece of paper, knowing it represented money that I could not collect because there was no real company or real company bank account.

Still, undeterred, I pressed forward, each time looking for bigger sized jobs, and accepting all the little work too. Bismarck worked with me on the waste management jobs we found, and he also learned to help me in the fumigation business too. On one of the jobs we did, we used a chemical that burns one's skin on contact, and of course I was unable to offer any proper protective clothing. That night we kept having to wash our skin and stay wet to stop the fiery burning sensation. Much of the risk involved in doing the fumigation work was overlooked. It was only many years later as I expanded my knowledge of the fumigation and waste management industries and studied public health issues that I realized how hazardous the work was in those early days, and how little regard we had for our own health and safety. A scarf or rag draped over our mouths and noses sufficed instead of proper ventilated masks. While we took a modicum of care with mixing and storing chemicals, it is a fact that back then, our small-small operations would have failed all occupational health standards.

Fumigants were, and are, highly toxic. When I started working for Kodjo's father, and later as I started my own business, I don't believe we were adequately informed of the full dangers. Had we been, I am not sure it would have mattered because we were hard pressed to make a living. In fact, the entire industry in Ghana was only gradually becoming more regulated at the time. There were many instances of mislabeled or cheap pesticides reaching the market, along with the damaging practices of Western markets disposing of adulterated insecticides and chemicals in Africa, where no one paid attention. Even though Ghana had instituted pesticide control and management legislation in 1996, it was closer to 2003 when pesticide registration processes became enforced.

Still, my determination to increase my savings persisted, and when I found a place to sleep at night, either in the classroom or at Forlonshor or with Ocansey, and when I was eating overripe fruit with Bismarck, life seemed much better. I was ready for a new phase in my life, one which involved a clear freedom plan.

8
Bleak times and unexpected misfortune

For more than a year, I lived my life in a strange state of limbo, not having a fixed abode, chasing after small jobs, attending church, keeping my homelessness secret from my family and acquaintances. Still, it felt as if the sacrifices were not being made in vain, because I could see everything shifting forward towards a better future, even if it was very gradual. However, there was a time when something happened that almost derailed everything – the dream, the hard work, my entire life.

I had been crisscrossing the streets and walking back and forth armed with my small pamphlets, going from house to house and shop to shop. On one of these days as I was walking a little further than my usual route, I saw some familiar faces nearby. They were men, coworkers who had worked alongside me at Kodjo's father's fumigation business, Sunrise International. The ones who had mocked my simple eating habits. They approached to strike up a conversation, and when they asked what I had been doing since I stopped working for Kodjo's father, I mentioned that I was winning souls. There was some truth in the statement because I was handing out my fumigation business flyers, winning souls for my business. I forgot the incident, and when they saw me on a few occasions again with my backpack and flyers, it even seemed they pitied me on the streets as an evangelist.

Nothing prepared me for what happened next.

Perhaps it is a good point to digress and talk of the relations between Ghana and Nigeria. Both these West African countries share a history of having had British colonial masters. Yet as the countries have engaged cooperatively to deal with post-independence turbulence and economic challenges, there have also been periods of deep political discord. Especially around immigration, in the 1980s and 1990s. On and off, Nigeria has expelled Ghanaians, and Ghana has deported Nigerians. None of that was on my mind when we came to Ghana. As an average Nigerian simply making my way in life and seeking opportunities within the West African region, my focus was always on business first, politics later. Despite that, I was subconsciously aware of the negative stigma attached to Nigerians around the world, which I guess one would politely term industrious even in an illegal capacity.

But none of that seemed relevant back then, when I was a young Nigerian man in Ghana, navigating opportunities to survive. That innocence all changed in an instant. The moment that my former boss at Sunrise International, Mr Odjor, found out that I was doing small fumigation jobs, he became incensed that I would start the same business. His animosity grew until it extended to his workers and his children and their associates, who were all angered that this Nigerian boy would dare step on their turf. And on that fateful morning, I rose early from the school classroom and headed to Ocansey's place to gather my fumigation materials.

I walked with a light step because I had a small job lined up, and with that money, I would be able to buy food. I fetched my fumigation machines from Ocansey's kiosk and brought them to the roadside, looking about for a taxi. Suddenly I saw Kodjo's brother Evans and a policeman walking towards me hastily. The policeman grabbed me by my pants waist, and started dragging me with him like I was a thief, telling me I was under arrest. The people standing by the roadside watching had that look. As if it was what they expected from a Nigerian, to be involved in some sort of criminal activity.

The policeman continued to pull and shove me, and I did my best to follow without resisting, unsure of what was to come next. Soon we were at Mr Odjor's house, the owner of Sunrise International, and I was thrust into a seat while the policeman and the others around me spoke in their Ghana language. After a while, Mr Odjor emerged from the house and confronted me, saying that if I wanted to work, it would have to be for him only. As he made his demands, I recalled how I had been so much better than all his other workers, showing up early to wash his vehicles, always volunteering for extra work on the job sites. All that effort for no gain, compared with being my own boss. I told him no; I would not return to work for him.

The man became livid, shouting that he would deal with me and that when he was done, I would not even recognize myself in a mirror. The others became agitated and insisted they should do what they had planned to do with me. Mr Odjor told me they would lock me up and no one would come for me; I would rot in a jail in Ghana. I knew his words to be true because who would come to my aid, a Nigerian accused of a crime. Soon I was taken to the police station where I was told that I was being charged with having stolen fumigation equipment from Sunrise International. Moreover, they added that Evans, Mr Odjor's son, claimed to have seen me taking money along with the equipment.

From that point, events blurred into a state of unreality. The policemen started noting down charges in a folder; they told me to undress, and they removed all my belongings – including my watch and my phone. They made me move behind the counter and suddenly I was placed into a cell, hardly comprehending what was going on. My overriding thought was that I was going to lose that client and job where I was supposed to be that day. Somewhere in my mind I thought this police station drama would all end and I would be able to make it to the client so that I did not let them down. And then it was evening, and I was still in the cell, and no one was talking to me, even when I tried to tell them I had been falsely accused.

My tears started to fall freely, and nothing made sense anymore. All those months and months of starving and sacrificing and saving to make a small amount of money, from honest hard work. I wept bitterly, until the other men in the cell started asking me what I had done and why I was locked up. I told them I did not know how I could be locked up for a crime I did not commit. A few of them drew closer and started advising me, saying I must find someone I know and call them, let them come and pay some money to get me released. But who did I know who would have money to buy my freedom? My situation felt entirely hopeless. I just sat there. As darkness fell, the cell inmates jostled for a place to lie or sit – there were more than twenty of us in a space meant to hold a quarter that number. We found there was a tribal chief with us in the cell, and he was given the only bed. The rest of us eventually lined up like sardines on the cement floor, and even though I believed sleep would not come, in the end through sheer exhaustion I drifted off.

When morning came it brought with it even more despair for my situation, because I had no idea what to do or where to start to gain my freedom. The station commander started his rounds, and when he got to our holding cell, he asked each of us in turn why we were locked up. When my turn came, I told him I did not know what crime I had committed. He looked over at the CID officer handling my case and said they should talk privately. It seemed he felt there was something untoward about my arrest, but I was left to wait some time before he returned. He then told me he had tried repeatedly to reach Mr Odjor so that he could come to the station and provide details for a charge statement. Either Mr Odjor did not answer his calls or had said he would not come to the station because later in the day, the station commander told me that he could not release me unless I paid bail. He asked if I knew anyone that I could call.

At that point I felt so abandoned, so distrustful, because it felt that all the people who knew me in the Osu community had allowed this to happen. I thought hard about anyone else I knew who would perhaps be willing to help me out. Then a name came to mind, there was a woman, named Madam Pat, and I had met her at the Tullow offices in Labone and done work for her at her house in Teshie. She had been so kind to me then. I asked if I could phone her and began praying that she would take my call, worried that if she heard there was this Nigerian man in police custody, she would not want to have anything to do with it. Thank God, Madam Pat answered the call, listened to me, and came to the police station. She gave me a character reference, telling the police officers that I had proven myself trustworthy time and again, even when they had left money about in their Tullow offices, I had never touched a cent of it. Madam Pat signed my bail, and the police officers told me I would have to return to the station the next day. When I did come back the following day, the station commander asked if I wished to press charges because it was frivolous and illegal for people like Mr Odjor to waste police time all because he supposedly wanted to teach me a lesson.

I had no desire to press any charges, even though they said I could if I so desired. I could not see the purpose of any court case; all I knew was that I needed to start seeking clients again. My hunger to become financially free had been fueled by this negative experience.

9
Winning and losing and learning all the time

Much of my business progress was trial and error, and persistence in the face of odds. On a day, I went to the SSNIT (Social Security and National Insurance Trust) guest house – this was a government location, and the lady there asked me for my EPA certificate. I asked her what that was, and she explained that anyone who has a business working with pesticides or chemicals that can affect the environment had to have a special certificate that would be issued by the Environmental Protection Agency. She explained further that having such a certificate would be the best way for me to get business contracts with restaurants, shops, and hotels. She showed me where to find the EPA office, and I made my way there, not even sure what they would require of me. I walked in and asked for a certificate, and the man at the EPA desk was amused as he explained to me one did not simply get a certificate. I would need certain qualifications, I would need to show I had a proper place to store my chemicals, and my company would have to be properly registered.

Determined now with the knowledge that having a proper company was the only way ahead, I found out how to register a business in Ghana. I discovered first, that as a foreigner, I would need to have a Ghanaian partner to register the fumigation business. The people I knew best were in the church with me, and I reached out to three of them. Two offered to help; one was Ocansey, who had already been my friend helping with the business by printing the sales leaflets. I decided to register a pest control business with him called JNRS Pest Control Ltd – the name that had come to me earlier. (The other person who agreed to be my business partner was Bismarck, and much later I would register a second business – called Nissiguide – with him.) Ocansey was already able to see the potential of such a pest control business, and I knew he wanted to leave his job at Melcom one day and become his own boss. We agreed that he would handle all our business administration, and I would do the operational work. Ocansey had already supported me in small ways, and I believed we would be able to grow the business together.

It took a while and several visits to the registrar-general's offices before my company with Ocansey was registered – and I immediately opened a bank account, deposited that very first check I had received, and returned to the EPA office. Over time I have come to see this trait in myself, the willingness to try something even when I do not meet whatever requirements list there may be. It was the same with the EPA – I knew my qualifications were lacking, and I hardly had place to sleep myself let alone store chemicals safely. When I went back to the EPA office, I took the application form and filled it out to the best of my ability. The EPA staff listened to my impassioned pleas for a certificate and said I would need to talk to their boss, a certain Mr

Edward. Later in life I have been told that I have a high likeability factor – and even though I do not fully understand it, the truth is that people do tend to like me and find it easy to connect with me. Mr Edward appeared to like me instantly, and even though I did not have all the necessary things in place, he said he would make time to come inspect my set up.

The day I met up with Mr Edward to take him to Ocansey's house for the EPA inspection, which we had said was our workplace, I was sweating profusely. I knew we would get there, and the EPA man would see we stored our fumigation machine and chemicals in an inadequate kiosk that was frequently opened and closed for other purposes. I had made a small space that was separate in the kiosk, but my knapsack and the chemicals and the machine just stood on the ground. We arrived and he saw immediately it was a family house, not a business property. We walked slowly through Ocansey's family home, to the back where the plain kiosk stood in the yard, and I told him this was my storage place – even though it was filled with shovels and other garden shed stuff. All the while I recognized the look on Mr Edward's face – somewhere between kindness and bemusement. As we returned to his car, I prayed Mr Edward would see past all the ways my business fell short, and that he would see in me an enterprising young man who desperately wanted to succeed. Mr Edward climbed in the car and wound the window down, almost taking in the measure of the eager man before him as he did so. After a while he looked up at me, smiled, and said we should go back to the EPA office to collect my certificate. I thanked God for His goodness and mercy, and for Mr Edward's kind heart.

The woman I met at the SSNIT guest house had unknowingly become instrumental in my success, because once I understood that meeting compliance and regulatory standards mattered, it became a pillar for the way I built my businesses. There were still more things to learn about entrepreneurship, but knowing the importance of having the right paperwork was a significant game changer for me. With the company registered, I was able to return to a bank and take the registration documents with me to open a bank account. With the EPA certificate in my hands, I could approach hotels, restaurants, and companies armed with a critical piece of paper that few other pest control companies had in Accra. And everywhere I went, I flashed that certificate and my company credentials! It was my good fortune that the Food and Drugs Board in Ghana was also intensifying its efforts to make sure that public facilities complied with certain hygiene and health standards. So, I kept moving around, knocking on doors, seeking opportunities. The business was becoming more real each day, not just a money-in-pocket and hand-to-mouth set up. I now had a doorway to step through, to grow my fumigation and pest control business properly.

There was a lot of trekking on foot involved in those early days. I would walk from Osu to 37 Military and on to Shangri La and Spanner Junction, moving even to East Legon, all in one day. It was around fourteen miles, and by foot it would take me four to six hours to complete the loop and hand out proposals and flyers along the way. One day, I received a call from the Managing Director of a new luxury apartment complex that was being built near the airport – a place called Polo Court. He had gotten my number from a flyer somewhere, and said I needed to be at his office by 8 am the next morning. Because I didn't have transport, or money to get a ride, I knew I would have to leave extra early to walk the two hours to get there. I was still sleeping in the classroom, so rising early was already a set habit, and the prospect of a job made the early morning walk easier. But that didn't reduce the tropical humidity of Accra, and I was sweating heavily as I got closer to the Polo Court property. I found a big shady tree, wiped myself off and waited for a few minutes to cool down before I headed to the location.

A driver was waiting to take me to the MD's office. I walked in confidently with my prepared pitch, introduced myself and said how much I would charge to fumigate the property. The MD looked at me and said it cost too much, and he would not pay that amount. My confidence tumbled and, in my head, I was saying, "Please, you must give me this job because I just walked two hours to get here, and I need the money." But when I spoke, I focused on the service I could offer, with good quality chemicals. The MD remained resolute and insisted he would find someone else who would be cheaper. I did quick calculations when he said the amount that he would be willing to pay and realized that once I factored in the cost of transporting my fumigation equipment, and the cost of chemicals, I would be running at a loss. I tried to persuade the MD to cover costs only of me doing the work, and again he refused, saying he would get someone who took less money. I was devastated, not only that I had put in all that time and effort to get to Polo Court, but also because I had no backup job, no way to bring in any immediate income. I realized how much I had been counting on getting this work, and yet, I could not bring myself to do the work for less than it was worth. I left.

Dejected, very angry with myself. Not getting that job was a disastrous blow. As I walked back towards Osu, I weighed up the fact that not having work meant not having anything, not even a job with Kodjo's father to fill the gaps. All connections there had been severed after the police arrest incident. Soon I found myself walking past another building site, where they were erecting the new Holiday Inn hotel. On a whim, I entered the site area and was met by a woman who asked who I was looking for. I said loudly that I was there to meet with the MD. She said, "Oh, you want to see Mr Bahige Torbay," and I said yes, not even knowing who this man was or how to say his name properly. She picked up her phone and called the site engineer, who was managing site operations. He was busy up on the seventh floor of this building that was under construction, and he came down all those flights of stairs, because there was no working elevator yet. To this day I'm not sure what went through his mind when he saw this tall, slim, grinning Nigerian in front of him. He greeted me and asked my name, and I introduced myself as Ike who had a fumigation company, handed him my printed flyer, and said I wanted to come spray their site for them.

Mr Bahige bobbed his head and told me, no, that was not how they did things there. He explained that I would need to submit a proposal for their consideration. I had no idea what a proposal looked like and was happy when Mr Bahige provided some further instructions, that he imagined I would want to measure up the place to be able to see how much insecticide I would need to use for the dimensions of the space. He assigned someone to take me around, and I made a good show of taking measurements, length and breadth and height, and writing down room sizes of the building and offices that housed the construction work. At least all my good math skills Mr Smith had taught me were coming in handy! I went back to my school classroom, sat at a desk, and pulled out my papers to deliver all these enthusiastic mathematical equations. Looking back now I laugh at my efforts with my limited understanding, my small grasp of the scope of business. You do the best within your constraints.

The following day I went back to Mr Bahige, and he said no, no, no! Then by God's grace he sat down with me and guided me through the process of how one prepares a business proposal, and what documents need to be attached. Armed with this new information, I started making my way back to Osu. As I walked, I remembered there was a man named Mr Charles, who was very knowledgeable about business, and he had worked with Sunrise International before on preparing such proposals. I took a chance and went to Mr Charles's house at Airport Residential, which was nearby. I told him I had a big business contract lined up but that I needed to know how to draft a good proposal. He graciously went with me to Holiday Inn, then helped me draft my proposal, and even added my company name. I took it back to Mr Bahige and that was how I started working for Holiday Inn in Accra. Up until today, they are still one of my clients.

It seems all my business opportunities started the same way, where I did not have the relevant knowledge, the relevant documentation, the relevant expertise, even the relevant equipment. But I had a heart and soul and a willing attitude to learn. For the first time I was confident; I had everything I needed to expand my business reach and make sales to new, bigger clients. Now all this time, I had still been living without a proper place to stay, sleeping most nights in the classroom, and sometimes over at Ocansey's place. But I had been doing what I knew best, sacrificing and saving, and I had reached a point where I had gathered enough money to be able to pay rent. In Ghana, as in Nigeria, when you rent accommodation, you are required to pay the full one or two years in advance to secure a lease. There were no month-by-month rentals, although these days the law states a landlord may only request six months in advance. So back then, it was a big sum of money that was required, and I had finally managed to save enough.

I was still at the classroom, and at this time Bismarck still had no idea I was staying there, in the room that doubled as our church venue. I was therefore looking forward to renting a place of my own, but everywhere I went, the landlords would have reasons why they did not want to rent to a young Nigerian man. They said we caused trouble, that we are a nuisance, and had all manner of excuses. There was a young Ghanaian woman in the neighborhood, and she was living with her boyfriend. She assured me that with their help, I would be able to get a place to rent. The plan was that she would go in my stead and set up a rental agreement, and that I would then stay in the property. I took all the money I had saved for rent and gave it to her. And she disappeared with it. This young lady ran away with my rent money.

Can you imagine, I was already packed and ready to leave the classroom, psychologically free from the stigma of being homeless because I was meant to move into my new living place that day. I called the young woman's number so she could come meet me to show me where the rented place was, and she never answered. I tried again, throughout the day, feeling more desperate, more fearful each time I dialed her number and got no reply. Sleeping in the school that night was one of my longest, hardest nights ever. My salvation from being homeless was cut short. I cried that night. This selfish young girl did not know how much I had suffered, how much I had sacrificed and given up, how much I had endured, to get that rent money together.

After a week, then a month, I gave up calling her number. I continued to stay in the classroom, doing my best, living as I could, and I started saving all over again. I felt emotionally lost, unable to focus on anything else happening in the world other than trying to take my business forward, job by job, and at night, burying myself in books and more books and reading, reading. That was my mental escape from the confines of a classroom that once had sheltered me, but now felt like an endless trap. Somehow all the practical advice in the books that I found kept me on track, urging me to save and save and plan and invest and stay focused on my future. I planned to buy better machines, I needed to sharpen my mindset, I wanted to further my education – that is how I stayed focused. Anything that would make tomorrow a better day, was good for me.

10
Going offshore and growing rich

As it turned out, my tomorrows started to improve in a surprising way. It was as if all the small connections, the stumbling blocks, and the wrong paths were suddenly straightening and coming into line. Sometimes we don't see the bigger journey unfolding because we are focused on the steps just in front of us. That is how it was for me. I took everything day by day and made sure that we put customer satisfaction high on our list. In my business journey it seemed that opportunities kept flowing as long as I could prove I was capable. I also never stopped being willing to do the work myself. I would tell myself, forget when you are feeling tired, and just start doing the work. Hard work is unlikely to kill you. What kills your spirit is when you work hard in a low paying job all the time, and you don't have a plan for how to move from one level of life to another. And I always had a plan.

One Saturday morning, Bismarck and I had donned our best suits – in fact, we were both wearing our finest because we were attending a wedding. The church was full of people, and we were seated in the congregation enjoying the joyful atmosphere, with flowers and ribbons and smiles all around us. I noticed my phone starting to vibrate, and as I slipped it out my pocket, I could see it was one of my clients who worked at Tullow Oil. I made my way out of the church hall and answered the call – the client had a problem, as some trees had been trimmed and were now blocking part of their road. I motioned to Bismarck and told him we had a job waiting. My loyal work partner didn't hesitate, and soon we were both in my Kia Sportage making our way to the client.

When we got to the site, there were a lot more branches than I had expected, even the roadside gutter was full. These open gutters are full of filth and have quite a stench. Bismarck and I puzzled a few moments to figure out how to load the trimmed branches into the back of the Kia. Then, with a plan in mind, we took one look at our beautiful outfits. Off our suits came, folded neatly, and set aside – and there we were removing branches from the road and gutter and stacking them in the vehicle. Looking back, I realize that these were some of my best moments. Bismarck had that same mind, do the work, and forget what people around you may be thinking. This willingness to always be there for my clients who worked at Tullow, paid off in several ways. There was the time Madam Pat bailed me out at the police cells. There was also the time in 2008 when we were introduced to Ocean Rig, an oil drilling company that had signed a US$700 million contract with Tullow Oil to drill wells for Ghana's new ocean oil fields.

The Ocean Rig offices were in Accra, and we started doing our routine waste collection and fumigation. We submitted invoices, got paid, all was going well. One night – because that was when Bismarck and I did almost all our work – we were parked outside the Ocean Rig offices and had just finished hauling their trash bins to load the rubbish into our truck. A Landcruiser drove by us, slowing to look at what we were doing, and we didn't think much of it as we continued to do the job. We finished and left. The following day when I stopped by the Ocean Rig offices to drop off our monthly invoice, I was pulled aside. The man who came over to talk with me had Scandinavian features – tall, light haired, lean, and well built, and he had a no-nonsense air about him. He said his name was Martin Holmström, and he asked if I had been the one handling their bins the night before. I responded yes, unsure if there had been a problem, and he walked off. Then, while I was standing in the accountant's office the phone rang, and he said to me, Mr Holmström wants to talk to you. I took the phone and Martin simply said they had an air conditioner that wasn't working, and that he wished me to attend to it, but he didn't want to deal with me, so I should handle the matter with the accountant.

And so, I did. Well, I knew nothing about air conditioning systems, but I happened to know some people who worked on them at Holiday Inn. I headed over to the hotel and found an AC technician, and we came back to the Ocean Rig offices, checked to see what was wrong and found the problem. It required a spare part, which I went to purchase and then returned. In less than an hour, the AC was working again. I informed the accountant of the cost, and he told Martin that the AC was fixed. Before I could leave, Martin stepped out his office to tell me he was almost shocked because he had been trying to get maintenance repairs done, and each time had been given the same story. People would show up, look at the problem, tell him they would come back the next day, then seldom show up until a few days later. That day he informed everyone in the Ocean Rig offices that henceforth I would handle all their maintenance issues.

Our business plan evolved. Suddenly I was doing fumigation, waste management, plumbing, painting, air conditioner servicing – all manner of maintenance and repairs. The only thing we weren't doing was housekeeping and cleaning, as they already had a contracted company for that. One time, they had an issue over at the Tema Oil Refinery and the technicians weren't available. No problem – "Send Ike" was the message that came down from Martin. I headed to the refinery and discovered that a particular seal was broken, which meant it was possible the oil had been compromised. I instructed them to replace the seal and the oil and let the main office know it had been done. Problem, solved. I continued working this way, providing maintenance services as and when they were needed.

It was a few months of this when Martin called me to his office again. This time, he mentioned that he wanted me to go complete some training. He didn't tell me anything other than where and when the course was being conducted, and that it would be good for me to complete it. A few days later I headed to the place he mentioned, the Regional Maritime University, and saw it was a Basic Offshore Safety Induction and Emergency Training course that cost almost US$2000, and which took around three weeks to complete. I immediately turned and left. In my head, there was no way I could justify the expense – plenty money that I could not afford – nor the time. A few months later, Martin asked if I had completed the course yet. When I said no, he didn't say anything. A few weeks later I bumped into the rig manager, and he said, "Ike, I thought Martin was going to ask you to do the BOSIET course. They want you to go out and do the fumigation on the rigs because they don't like the company that's got the contract now."

My mindset shifted instantly; now doing the US$2000 course was an investment, not a cost. I read up a bit more about it, that the course was designed to provide the necessary skills to handle a variety of emergency scenarios working offshore. I had never imagined that I would find myself heading off into the ocean to do fumigation work, and I was going to miss the opportunity if I didn't find a way to do the initial offshore safety training, emergency response training, and all the necessary assessment requirements to be able to work in the offshore oil and gas industry. I started the following week and finished the course, got my BOSIET certification, and returned with it in my hand to show Martin. Within weeks, the investment in getting certified paid off. Martin gave me my first offshore fumigation work.

I never knew anyone could be paid the amount of money they were paying me for a single job, in dollars. It was a whole new world, with helicopter flights out to ocean rigs that were anchored in deep waters offshore. Where attention to detail was a matter of survival for those living and working on the rigs. Everyone did everything with technical precision; there were regular safety checks, and it was easy to see why – the changing weather, the constant ocean waves – much more challenging than any factory I had seen operating on dry land. It was a bit like compound living, with shared baths and rooms with bunkbeds and the cafeteria where we all ate together. I would bunk down with the other rig workers, staying on the rig for a few days depending on in and out flight schedules, even though the fumigation process probably took less than a day. And I enjoyed it. My mechanically minded logic was fueled in that oil rig environment as I learned more about how oil rigs operated. Soon, Martin added the Takoradi fumigation rotation to our workload. This meant traveling up the Ghana coastline about 140 miles, to their oil rig set up in Sekondi-Takoradi.

The work with Ocean Rig brought a new line of business services, doing their maintenance. Over time even the maintenance contract expanded into more technical problem solving. Martin again called me to his office one day and told me they had a new contract available if I was interested in making more money. They wanted us to start servicing the risers – these are the pipes that the drilling head goes through, connecting the rig operations to the ocean floor. The pipes must be regularly serviced and maintained between drilling operations, and this work needs to be done onshore. Once a well had been completed and drilling was finished, they would bring the risers back to shore. I employed six technical workers at the Takoradi site to do the maintenance and opened a new business bank account there.

Martin Holmström became my teacher without actively teaching me. In him I found someone whom I could observe and learn from his actions. Like when I showed up at his office and he would remove his eyeglasses, push his laptop aside, and focus fully on his conversation with me. Martin saw me, my hunger, my passion, the grit in me. He lifted my confidence to new levels. I was no longer dried-out like driftwood; instead, Martin made me feel like I was a well-oiled a piece of wood that had soaked in much of life's hard lessons and I was ready to be sparked. Up until today, I have never met anyone who believed in me as much as Martin did. His actions showed me how I was a useful and valuable cog with skills that could slot into a big machine. He took risks with me, knowing I did not have the requisite experience. He set a task, raised the bar, expected me to learn – and he believed in me. Some days Martin would invite me to lunch, and I would sit down with his European colleagues who would be genuinely interested in me, asking what I was doing and how I was learning new things. They went out of their way to be nice to me, to give me opportunities. All the while it felt good, yet it also felt unbelievable to me, and part of me wondered when it would suddenly end.

As I managed the Ocean Rig money coming in – thousands of dollars each month – I would pay everyone working for JNRS, and I would put almost all my fixed salary portion into my bank account, leaving it untouched. The work required that I had to be in Takoradi once a week to oversee the maintenance and to verify that all safety and security measures were being implemented. So, I watched as all the young men spent the money they were earning, some on cars, others bought land, one bought a place for his girlfriend. I held onto the money in my account, reluctant to spend anything. But I was no longer homeless. I secured a place to stay; it was on Bush Road, a dilapidated rented room with an outdoor toilet and bathroom, just the bare necessities. The feeling that all the business success might go away, remained. It compelled me to keep all our multiple revenue streams going, to keep working like the future was not assured.

Throughout this time, Ocansey from church had remained my Ghana business partner in JNRS, and he had been supporting me with administration. Both of us saw that our revenue streams were growing, and business was expanding, enough for Ocansey to make the decision that he would leave his job at Melcom, the retail store. We agreed he would move to Takoradi and begin to play a more active role in running the business there while I concentrated on the physical operations and oversight of work that had to be done in Accra and Tema.

The Takoradi side of our contracts was almost all profit because Ocean Rig covered all expenses, from transport and accommodation to maintenance materials and supplies. Money was flowing into our account and business was going well. Unexpectedly I heard from the Takoradi workers that they had not been receiving their wages. I immediately called Ocansey and asked what was going on. He told me he had taken money from the business account to help someone at church who was having financial problems. In West Africa it is not unusual for business owners to use their company accounts as a pocket they dip into when they want money for personal needs. I was very against this practice because it would only lead to financial problems in future. Ocansey and I argued about his use of the money; he felt aggrieved that he could not have independent decision-making power over the revenue we made. In my mind I was clear; business money was to be used for business purposes only.

Our debate went on for months, with the discussions becoming more heated. Perhaps my own approach to our business problems was wrong. Maybe I had not explained the revenue side well enough to Ocansey, and maybe I had been hard in my manner. I was ruthlessly clear that we would not use our JNRS account to solve money woes for church people. This annoyed Ocansey and subsequently he quit going out to find other clients and stopped trying to grow the Takoradi business. Instead, he said he was staying at home to pray over issues that mattered. We could no longer communicate properly. Eventually we realized we were at a partnership stalemate, and we approached the one person we felt would be able to help: Pastor Seth, the church man who had once kept me fed with bananas. In his presence we met a couple of times to talk, each presenting our own case as he listened. I had entered these mediation conversations believing we would find a way forward. And when Pastor Seth took a sheet of paper, tore it in half and handed us each a piece, asking us to write down whether we wanted the partnership to continue, I wrote YES. Ocansey wrote NO. Our partnership ended.

From the early days when Ocansey and I had merely had business pamphlets and big aspirations, we now had a solid business with assets. I opted to walk away from JNRS Pest Control Ltd, giving the Takoradi operations and assets to Ocansey, except for Ocean Rig. They remained as my client, and Martin would not have had it any other way. Ocansey kept the vehicles we had, the equipment in Takoradi and all the money that remained in the bank account. I kept the fumigation and waste management clients in Accra, and the assets we had there. Still, to register another business in Ghana I needed a new Ghana business partner. It was an easy decision, I knew immediately who I would ask – Bismarck, who had hauled trash bins and washed chemicals off his skin, who had saved me from electrocution and who worked with a tireless and generous heart. Together we launched a new company in April 2012, called Nissiguide Pty Ltd.

Business grew, and I grew as an entrepreneur too. It was a year when many things changed, including that for the first time in

Ghana, I was now able to buy a property near to the airport. One night I saw a streetlight shining in an area that was mostly small subsistence farms, so I knew they had started to build houses there. I found a piece of land for sale that was close to a river, and where everything was lush with life. Using my Ocean Rig earnings, I built a small house in two months – it was rough on the outside and the windows didn't have security. But I now had my own bedroom, a small kitchen, and an indoor bathroom. Oh, and I bought an excellent bed with the most comfortable mattress! So, in some way, I had come to Ghana for the promise of an oil deal that never materialized. Instead, I had built a business that grew from oil money anyway. Life is interesting.

11
Navigating to new opportunities

One of my favorite memories of working with Ocean Rig is of my first helicopter ride out to the rig, and my initial experiences there. Bear in mind that my whole life was largely land bound in a warren of closely stacked compound houses, and the idea of climbing into a flying object that would carry me over a wide-open ocean made me feel nervous. First, I travelled with the crew from Accra to Takoradi and we headed to the helicopter pad. In the preboarding process, I watched as each person stepped onto a scale and their weight was called. Later I would find that it was part of controlling the load. The oil rig men ahead of me, one weighed over 200 pounds, the other around 180 pounds. I stepped on; the machine registered my scant weight, not even 100 pounds. I watched carefully how the men boarded, where they held, how they sat, and I followed suit. Soon we were up and flying over that deep vast ocean, and I was praying we would not drop out of the sky!

The rig was much bigger than I had expected, it was an entire operational factory run by many people, busy all the time. As we exited the helicopter we were met by a health and safety officer who said we needed to do an induction. His British accent was so thick, I could not understand half of what he was saying, and whenever he asked a question, I simply said yes along with all the men around me. Once we were settled and I had a chance to look around, the one thing I really enjoyed was seeing people work without supervision. Each person was moving about, doing a task, working efficiently and independently, and yet collectively everything functioned seamlessly. My next amazing experience was the food. Like every three hours, there would be some sort of food. You start a shift with breakfast at 6 am, and by 9 am you have a hearty snack, then at 12 pm it is officially lunch time, and 3 pm they are coming with another snack. Dinner, that was a full meal served again at 6 pm. Work, eat. Work, eat. Can you imagine how that was for someone like me!

There was another benefit to being on the oil rig, because in downtime you would be able to call back to people you knew on land. I called my family, I called friends, I even called women I had recently met and who I wanted to impress. I would tell everybody I had traveled, and they would ask where, and occasionally I would laugh and say, "Norway" because that's the international dialing code that would be reflected. But I never joked about the work that I had to do. Everything required focus, attention to safety, and I did what I was supposed to do properly. In the evening, sometimes I would sit outside and watch the peaceful sea. It was a good time. Being on the rig, I was often lucky enough to be alone in a cabin and after work I would watch movies and relax. I never saw the danger and challenges of rig work, although I knew it was risky work. For me, it was about good food, good money, good work and good times.

When I had to leave the rig on my very first trip, I spent the day packing my stuff, getting ready to go. When it was time, we were called to prepare for boarding. I remember we watched a safety video again. In that moment I experienced a deep sense of gratitude because I was not meant to be on the rig. You see, I did not have a proper work permit back then. I always tell people, "Just try." Back in Takoradi, I was aware that my work papers were not in order, but I still got in the line, got weighed and got on the helicopter. Nobody asked me for my work permit. I was lucky because I tried. Later I would sort the work permit out, yet that very first time, I took a chance.

"Just try" was a strategy that had worked for me before. Our very first waste management job, where we collected trash from the private residence of the Tullow manager, the early days we had made do with help from the boys who pull hand carts. It was a short-lived solution. With Bismarck then helping me, I devised a new plan. I went out and bought big black trash bags, and the two of us would collect trash from our clients and re-bag it to disguise it. Then I would leave Bismarck standing with a bunch of these black sacks while I went off in search of a taxi with a big trunk, and we would load it in the back and drive around until we found a big dumpster and we would offload the trash there. As they say, necessity is the mother of invention, or in our case, desperation gave rise to disguising and dumping refuse in ingenious ways.

Mr Bahige from the Holiday Inn was a tremendous help when it came time for me to get my own car. He sold me his old Kia Sportage for a low price. I fixed the seats, made some small repairs, and it worked well for my needs. How I learned to drive was a crazy thing. Up to that point I had always made use of a driver who would come take me around and then on a day, the man said he did not feel like going when I needed to leave. I got in the driver's seat, sparked the engine, and started to drive. And so, my "just try" spirit instantly gave me more freedom. I never went to driving school at all; everything I needed to learn, I discovered along the way. As a result, Bismarck and I switched from using taxis to using the Kia Sportage. Having a vehicle spurred me on to find new clients, especially restaurants and shop owners, identifying potential clients when we found uncollected trash on their premises. Our waste collection services gradually grew.

What I did not know at the time was that waste management was heavily regulated in Accra, and that waste management companies each had specific zones assigned to them, where they collected garbage during the day. Our efforts to obtain a zone permit failed – we could not afford to stuff envelopes in decision-making hands, and zones were linked to government incentives, which made them extra hard to come by without the right connections. However, many of these zoned companies would have equipment or staffing issues and fail to do rounds regularly. Soon the companies that had zones where I was operating noticed they were losing clients. At the time, the issue was not addressed at a business-to-business level; instead, companies that were unhappy with Nissiguide would go to the Metropolitan Assembly and lay a complaint against my business. By chance I discovered a sort-of useful loophole. Any client who was not satisfied with the efficiency or services provided by the waste management company which held the zone permit, was allowed to decline those services, provided they removed the trash themselves. Nissiguide stepped into the gap. It was a tricky scenario, and we opted to work at night, which had the benefit of less traffic on the roads and kept diesel costs low, as well as the cover of darkness to remove trash for our clients.

Our strategy was to optimize routes and the proximity of clients, allowing us to drive less, save fuel, and work in limited areas, while having higher profit margins. On one occasion when we were taken to court because we were collecting waste from a restaurant, it was the restaurant owner herself who sat in court to testify on our behalf, and we watched as she showed the judge pictures of the rat-infested premises caused by trash not being collected by the zoned company. The owner was very clear saying that she wanted her trash to be collected daily, and that she wanted it to be done in the late hours of night when her restaurant was closed so as not to affect her business. She informed the judge that we were the only company that could offer the service she needed to run a hygienic restaurant. Fortunately, the judge agreed, telling the zone complainant that it was evident they could not do the job and that they were frustrating the people who could do it – and the judge threw the case out of court.

A different waste management company opted for a strategy where they took one of our other clients to court. Most likely because they believed the client would not want the hassle of a court case and that they would terminate our services. Usually when the client was the subject of the case, Nissiguide would tell them we would be standing by to hear how they wanted us to proceed, or if we should cease. Almost invariably, the clients would always return to us, even if it was a few months later. It was also how we came to include the loophole discussion when we signed future clients, informing them that in their dealings with the Metropolitan Assembly, they should specify that they would manage their own waste disposal processes, and that we were being hired not to collect, but rather to dispose of that waste.

In time, Nissiguide became a repository for many of the customer focus lessons learned in Nigeria. For example, we made sure that we could do the work when our clients wanted us to do it and we kept our contracts flexible. That flexibility extended to the relationships too. If clients were feeling a financial pinch, we would adjust collection schedules or services to get them through their tough times. When clients wanted daytime collections, we would pass by first thing in the morning when we had completed our night rounds, or we would do collection after we returned from the dumping site late afternoon. One of our other advantages was our personal availability. Many of the zoned waste management companies were so huge and impersonal, and hardly any had customer care lines. My clients signed contracts with me and had my phone number directly, and I always answered their calls. I would bring my invoices to them personally, and that was a time to build closer relationships.

My relationship with Ocean Rig allowed me to see more sides of how businesses work, especially at a scale where international economic forces are at play. Whoever would have imagined that from the poverty of life in Port Harcourt, now I was seeing wealth from a global scale. In the early days, Ocean Rig's presence in Ghana was as a fresh entrant into a newly discovered oil market. There weren't many rigs around, and the cost was exorbitant – I cannot recall exactly, but I think Tullow Oil was paying Ocean Rig around a million dollars a day for services. Ocean Rig's presence in Ghana was also very low key – there were no billboards or big advertisements. You would enter their offices and find an Ocean Rig business sign almost obscured on a small wall. It baffled me that a company which made so much money could exist without a big, branded presence. It was business thinking at a different level.

As time passed, rigs that had been drilling in other oceans started heading to West Africa to cash in on Ghana's new Jubilee Field oil wealth. Ocean Rig operated a semi-submersible drilling operation; now it was surrounded by these big modern drill rig ships that were more cost efficient and could offer Tullow better pricing terms. Soon Ocean Rig would leave the waters off Ghana and head to Cote d'Ivoire. It was replaced by two new drill ships, Olympia and Stena Forth. I watched all of this in real time, how Ocean Rig's revenue virtually halved overnight with new entrants into the drilling market. It made me question the sense of comfort I had started to develop around Nissiguide's multiple revenue streams. Yes, there were fumigation and waste management contracts, even maintenance and engineering contracts – but it could all come to an end. My head said it would be a good time to improve my living arrangements beyond the chamber and hall rental I had. But my gut said I needed to start saving again, putting aside as much as I could, and living only off what was necessary.

There was still no master plan in how I was doing business, everything was emerging. From oil rigs in ocean waters to blue ocean business thinking – I was seizing and making opportunities, and all these little steps to differentiate our Nissiguide services were succeeding in making the competition irrelevant. Except that we remained constrained to a niche market while I watched hundreds of houses and urban complexes springing into being in a rapidly growing lower middle income class Ghana. There was a point where I felt that this potential market was worth exploring. Soon I discovered it wasn't a viable proposition because homeowners did not use bank orders to pay for services. They preferred paying in cash – which resulted in a collections headache – or if they opted to use mobile money, you were still at their mercy for when they felt like paying. I realized that one of my business principles was to have control over both revenue and expenses, and collecting household waste didn't allow for that.

All in all, I had come to understand that refuse collection is reliable, predictable, and cash flow can be planned; yet in a market constrained by bureaucracy, growth is limited. I could see the future where there would be greater need in waste management as the complexity of refuse collection would eventually exceed the supervisory capacity of the Metropolitan Assemblies. These days I see many more individual operators plying the trade because the big, zoned companies have grown tired of waiting for government to make good on payments. Four years ago, I was weighing up business options in a competitively zoned industry. As an entrepreneur, it began to feel to me that Nissiguide was heading to a plateau. Our compaction trucks had been a big investment, our business was stable. Restaurants had become a primary customer segment, and experience proved that most restaurants have a five-year shelf life – but as some closed, others would open. We had a steady customer base, and it was good, but not enough. Soon I found the niche that brought Nissiguide into meeting urban growth needs in Accra. We did not have to go door to door to sign up individual homeowners if we focused instead on apartment blocks and complexes – and signed up the landlords as our clients. I had found a new, growing customer segment, but I knew things change.

Whatever was happening in my small business world, I paid close attention to what was happening with my clients too. Martin Holmström had told me Ocean Rig was leaving Ghana, and I anticipated that our contracts would scale down too. Then on a day I received a call from a foreign number, and when I answered, a secretary told me that Mr Holmström wanted to speak with me. As usual, Martin was to the point. "Ike, I am calling from Abidjan. Can you be here tomorrow?" Of course, I was going to be there! No problem – well, I had never been to Abidjan before, and I didn't speak French. But that hardly mattered because Martin had called, and I would find a way. That same evening, I found out there was an overnight bus to Abidjan, and I bought a ticket and arrived the following morning. I wanted to take a taxi to the Ocean Rig office, but it took forever to find a driver who spoke broken English – I must have asked about thirty of them! I called the office number and, luckily, they told the driver in French how to get to their location.

Martin greeted me in reception and asked if I could get my equipment to Abidjan because he wanted me to go offshore within the next three days. In my head I knew that I didn't know what it would take to get the equipment and chemicals over border crossings – and still I said yes to Martin. I would figure it out. Leaving the building I found my broken-English taxi driver and somehow communicated with him that I needed to get to a certain type of store that sold the things I would need. My idea was to have a backup plan in place if I couldn't bring my things from Accra. It's interesting how creative you become when you commit yourself to something. And my Ivorian taxi driver found the places I needed to go. Then I returned to Accra, packed all the equipment and chemicals in three big suitcases and bought a ticket to head back to the Cote d'Ivoire. I remember standing in front of the immigration officer, feeling slightly fearful as they checked my passport, knowing I didn't have the relevant work permit. Then I had a thought; the worst that could happen was I would be turned back, denied entry, and there was nothing to really lose, except to try.

"Are you Mr Onyema?" the immigration officer asked in his French accent, and when I said yes, he stamped my passport and waved me through.

Soon I was on an oil rig again, this time off the Ivorian coastline and it was all familiar and I went about doing everything I needed to do. I knew where to go, I knew how everything operated – it felt like I was in my work element. Even on one of the scheduled trips, when the flight back to shore was delayed for a few days and the Ocean Rig staff apologized for causing an inconvenience, I just smiled because being on the rig was one of my better life experiences. One time, our helicopter return was delayed and as we came to land at the airport, I saw my Accra flight taking off. The Ocean Rig staff booked me into the airport hotel; it had been recently built and everything still had that new shine. There was going to be a day before the next available flight to Ghana, and once I was in my hotel room, I couldn't help but think about my equipment and leftover chemicals that were packed in my suitcase. I headed downstairs and asked to speak to the manager, promptly offering to fumigate the hotel rooms for a reduced price. He agreed, and I made a quick US$2000 on my off day. *Just try* – it's probably my best business philosophy.

My connection with Ocean Rig took me to unexpected places, doing unplanned things, for good rewards. Later I would travel to Liberia and eat one of the best steaks I ever had in a hotel there, which seems so surprising because that country has been ravaged by decades of brutal civil war, and it is steeped in thick layers of poverty. Yet wherever you go in Africa, if you look just a little deeper, you will see there is opportunity upon opportunity.

12

If you want to go far, go together

Part of my plan to get to the next level in business and in life has always included investing in myself, and in my skills. As my entrepreneurial interests grew, I continued to read business books. At first, it would take me weeks, even months, to read a book and then to go through it again to gain a deeper understanding. In time, reading became second nature and I was averaging one new book every two weeks. Memoirs, biographies, business advice – always books that made me think. There was a point when I realized that my business interests would be best served if I furthered my education. I enrolled in Zenith University in Ghana for an Association of Chartered Certified Accountants qualification, and in 2014 completed my ACCA certification. It was where I discovered a natural affinity for finance and numbers, and so I decided to study through Oxford Brookes University, Online, UK, to get my BSc (Hons) in Applied Accounting, which I completed in March 2016.

Book learning and education eventually became pillars in my business growth. And my experiences with people like Mr Smith and Martin Holmström helped me realize that the road to future success may have speed bumps, but these could always be navigated as long as one remained curious and persistent. As my confidence grew, my approach to finding mentors changed; before, almost all my lessons were from books. Now I was eager to ask people I admired for entrepreneurial advice and guidance. It became part of my routine, when I stopped in to see customers – something I did regularly, even if I had to sit and wait for them to squeeze off five minutes for me from their busy schedules – then I would talk about how to do business better. Good leaders make time to mentor and encourage. In some instances, it was a book recommendation, such as when the managing director of Dalex Capital, Ken Thomson, told me to read *Blue Ocean Strategy*. I did, and it shifted my approach to Nissiguide's strategic direction.

Some of my mentors appeared in unexpected ways, like the night I stopped by an apartment building – Aspect Court – behind the US Embassy in Accra. It had a *To Let* sign on the wall, with a phone number. Because I was looking to connect with landlords and building owners, I dialled the number. The man who answered, Mr Eshun-Famiyeh Nuamah, would eventually become one of my most revered mentors, where I could say that knowing him has changed the course of my life more than once. He has a very respectful way of helping me rethink decisions; instead of telling me that I may be doing something wrong, he encourages me to think from different perspectives. At one point I was planning to abandon my ACCA studies, and it was the only time I recall Mr Nuamah being very direct with me. I argued that I should stop the studies because I was never going to become a practicing Chartered Accountant; I was only interested in being an entrepreneur. Mr Nuamah said that I should consider our friendship over if I dropped my studies. I continued, got certified, and realized that a university qualification is much more than book knowledge or a doorway to a career.

Yet it was also curious how people looked down on the work that I was doing, when I would say that I was working in fumigation and waste management. I once asked a friend if he would be interested in joining me in the work, because he needed a job, and I needed more workers. He told me that he had a university degree and so he could not become someone who picked up other people's trash. Perhaps because of where I came from, my own background of poverty and struggle, I never once felt too proud to do a lowly hard day's work. In fact, one of my next business ideas took me back to the markets. I met a young man who reminded me of myself with his entrepreneurial passion; he was providing microloans to street vendors, to the women who had food stalls at the roadside. It seemed a good business model where one could give a microloan for a few hundred cedis, and the market women who took loans would pay back in small amounts from their daily take, with a low interest rate. The women seldom defaulted, they were simply happy to have access to finance that allowed them to pay for their children's schooling, or cover house rent.

I partnered with this young man and made an investment so that the business could increase the number of microloans it was making to the market women. In the first few weeks, I saw a constant return. I was now also getting to be a mentor to a young entrepreneur, and the fact that I was having a social impact felt good. However, Nissiguide took a lot of my attention and in addition to my studies, soon I had removed my eyes off the business, and allowed this young man to manage our joint microloan venture by himself. Within a few months it was clear the business was in trouble. Upon investigating, I found out he had used part of the money he collected to put a down payment on a house in a development complex. He had fallen into the habit of taking money that was meant to be reinvested in making loans, and soon he could not keep up with his own debt payments. It was a mess, also because I felt badly for the market women whose loan repayments had been used fraudulently. For a short while I poured good money after bad, hoping to fix the business. In the end I accepted that it was not the kind of venture to entrust to someone if I didn't have time to control it all, so I walked away after losing around US$30,000 to that bad partnership experience.

By now, Nissiguide had one dedicated trash pick-up truck that I had been able to buy from a government auction. I recall spending many a late night and even some early mornings sitting at the mechanic's lot as he repaired our sole truck. I knew that if I left the mechanic to his own devices he would close and go home for the night. So, I would stay, even if it meant I had a sleepless night. Keeping that one truck on the road was the lifeblood of our business. This was where I needed to be very hands-on, making sure I knew of every potential vehicle problem. I don't imagine the clients ever knew what it took to ensure they would wake up to see all their trash bags had been collected.

Our Nissiguide customer retention is impressive; of the customers we have lost, it was because of their businesses closing. In a couple of instances, our contracts ceased when a company made a new hire, and that decision-maker had their own preferred waste management solution. The reality is that much of the time, trash collectors – the *bola* people – are an invisible layer the client never notices. We work quickly and quietly, efficiently moving in and out of places and taking trash burdens with us – no words are exchanged, no conversations or pleasantries, just seamless service that happens. Clients don't see the piles of trash or who picks it up; all they do is glance at an invoice and sign a check. That doesn't mean the work isn't without challenges. There are vehicles to maintain. There are rainy seasons when roads become bad, even impassable. There are challenges at the dumping site – if a bulldozer breaks down there it will disrupt the dumping schedule. Once in a while you will have two or three of your vehicles break down at once, despite your continued maintenance efforts. Life has shown me as much as one wants control, there are matters out of one's hands.

By the time the workload had become too much for Bismarck and I to manage on our own, I had found my next Nissiguide hire. It was Ben, the mechanic who did our truck maintenance and who lived close by. I suggested to him that as we did refuse collection after dark, he could work part of the day, rest in the late afternoon, and then give us a helping hand at night. He agreed, and that meant I could adjust some of the workload, with Bismarck handling fumigation jobs during the day while I went out prospecting for more clients, and the three of us covering waste pickup schedules at night. Our client numbers kept increasing and our collection terrain expanded. We needed more people.

Bismarck had a friend named JK, whom he had met cutting down trees on a side job. JK was physically strong, and that was an asset. He was working as a coconut seller during the day. Within a few weeks of joining Nissiguide, JK was able to quit selling coconuts because his nighttime job collecting trash paid better. JK didn't know how to drive, so we invested in training him and soon we had Ben and JK alternating as drivers – one week on, one week off. Now it became easy to grow our customer base because we would literally be driving and see people having piles of uncollected trash outside their businesses. We showed up, said we could dispose of their *bola*, asked them to try us out and soon we had more and more happy new clients. We stayed selective in these clients, almost like the cherries on a cake, we would cherry pick customers whose trash was cleanly bagged and easy to handle.

When it came to hiring other people to work for Nissiguide, I would first consider where people lived, how much money they needed for transport, and what it would cost to feed them. Transport cost money and meant possible delays for staff getting to work. I concluded it was best to hire people who lived close to where we were based. I am sure every entrepreneur eventually discovers that when you have people who work for you, then you increase your number of problems. I thought my hiring philosophy, inspired by the people I saw working without supervision on oil rigs, was a good way to reduce employee challenges. I had noticed with other waste collection companies that if their trucks ran into problems, the drivers would abandon the vehicles at the roadside and leave client trash to pile up. For Nissiguide, I instituted an employee practice that if you ran into an issue, even if it was at 2 am, you had to sort out the problem. If the vehicle broke down, you fixed it. If you couldn't get it to move, you found another way – using a taxi, whatever it took, but you always collected the customer's rubbish before the sun came up. As I brought on more staff, I decided to keep using the shift system, again like the oil rig schedules.

Our company culture also grew stronger. Bismarck and I already embodied the Nissiguide belief of whatever it takes, you must solve the problem for the client. We gradually began to operate like a more regular company, getting all our waste management workers to come in and sit down for a team meeting where we explained how business should work. Our motto became: *Find a way, fix it*. If the truck broke down in the middle of the night, then you repaired it, and if you couldn't, you returned to the office to take the second truck, and if that truck wasn't available, you used someone else's car to do the work. Find a way, fix it. Our way of doing business was to be seamless and invisible, with no clients ever having to think or stress about how we collected and disposed of the trash they created. It is still that way today.

Back then, in our team meetings, I would use the time to talk about safety awareness and savings behavior. To promote the investment habit I believed in, I would also encourage everyone to save some of their wages. Soon I started a new practice with all Nissiguide staff, telling them we could agree on an amount they would each use to buy a treasury bill, and that if they showed me the receipt, I would match their investment for them. Some did, others didn't. It evolved into a process where a few of them told me they wanted to buy land, including Bismarck and JK, and I became actively involved in their investment and wealth creation strategies.

Eventually the performance reviews I did with staff at Nissiguide were always tied to investment or future goals – something that continues to this day. Instead of talking about salary increments,

I would offer to help each person realize a financial goal – to buy land, to pay for schooling. It didn't work for everyone, but where some embraced it, they always saw longer term rewards. We kept growing and growing, and soon each driver had a team of four people working with them on a shift. My role also shifted – I became more of the office administration person, the one tasked with handling billing and customer service, also doing marketing and outreach. When administration peaked, I hired three more office staff. Our team meetings became more interactive – we would aim to meet twice a month, once to talk about occupational safety and review our incidents, the other time to brainstorm marketing and business ideas. We would listen to each other and give feedback, our main aim to help build up confidence and to create a sense of family.

It was in this time that we had another of our lowest points in the business. JK's truck broke down and the repairs were going to take much longer than we expected. Ben was out on his route in our only truck when he was involved in an awful accident. The driver of the other vehicle was a military man, and his vehicle was completely written off, and the man himself had a bad leg injury. Ben was adamant the military man had been at fault and caused the collision, and as it was late, there was also the fact that the man reeked of alcohol. However, the military man insisted that no civilian could require him to do a drunk driving test. It was also apparent to me that the military man feared losing his commission. In the end, our truck was badly damaged, but the military man's injuries were severe, and so we were compelled to pay for his surgery and hospitalization, as well as his vehicle that had been written off. This took all our money reserves, and we were running on empty, without a truck to work.

Yet that was only part of our hardship. Now we had no truck, and we had many, many customers depending on us, and our reputation was at stake. The unhappy customer phone calls started coming day after day, even as I tried to make different arrangements, hiring boys manually pulling carts, renting three-wheelers, trying to find people with cars that would load trash bags in the trunk, paying a high premium for fuel and time. I burned through most of the money I had saved finding ways to deal with call upon call upon call. It became impossible to keep up with our waste management collection, and I felt desperate enough to start randomly calling key clients, pleading for patience, even asking a few for a possible loan. Mr Nuamah was one of the people I called; he listened as I relayed our dire situation, and he asked what I needed to keep business going. My answer was simple – a new truck. He told me to wait, and that he would call me back. When he did, it was with an instruction to go to Rana Motors, one of the big vehicle dealerships in Accra, and to speak to Mr Essam Odeymat.

And so, I headed to this dealership with its gleaming sales floor and shiny new vehicles and asked for Mr Odeymat. Only then did I discover he was the managing director of Rana Motors, and I was ushered into his office. Hesitantly I explained that Mr Nuamah had told me to come meet with him. Mr Odeymat looked me over and asked, "What kind of truck would you like?" I replied that I would be willing to take whatever truck he would be willing to sell to me if I could pay the vehicle off over a period. Without any further due diligence or queries about my business,

Mr Odeymat and I discussed deposit and payment terms, and he put together a sales contract, and that day I left Rana Motors with a new truck and a lifelong debt of gratitude to Mr Nuamah for having vouched for me.

Ben had been concerned we would terminate him after the accident; instead, we used the experience to get better as a business. I became more particular about the drivers' skills and work attitude. We were clear there was zero tolerance for drinking and driving. We also encouraged the shift drivers to motivate their teams, because they needed to work as a close-knit unit, fast and efficiently throughout the night. You never know what is going to happen.

Overall, I began to understand why so many entrepreneurs fail in their first five years of business. Calamity strikes, it always will. And if you are prepared, then it may still take you some time to recover. If you are not ready for the disasters that befall businesses, you go down. I read somewhere that only the paranoid survive. It began to make sense, and I developed a healthy sense of paranoia around all aspects of the business – from competitors to environmental factors. This became part of my new drive to find other sources of income. Within Nissiguide we constantly thought of new revenue streams and weighed up customer segments. When we opted not to do household collection, we turned to estates and apartments instead. We avoided doing schools because they pay very little, and they generate a lot of waste. From hospitality and health businesses we expanded into factories and industrial premises that needed to get rid of waste we could manage.

The accident was a turning point in how I was becoming a better entrepreneur. It was a struggle to pay for that truck from Rana Motors, but we did. What I gained out of it was learning how to manage cashflow to the last cedi. I had to figure out how to survive again. It was all an operational strategy, responding to the paranoid thoughts in my head that what had come could easily be taken away. What our business needed most was diesel. I reached out to some of our steady suppliers and organized a two-month credit term. Take diesel now, pay later, save cash flow. Secure your operations, increase revenue, think about ways to expand business laterally, and invest in treasury bills.

Once again, business started turning around for Nissiguide and I could see we were on a path to financial freedom. The first years of my business, I had been working in it, being operational and tactical. Yet now I was gaining clarity about working on my business. It still came as a surprise that others were noticing Nissiguide too, and this attention led to something even more unexpected.

13
Seeds of transformation

It was just another normal sweltering day as I headed through the heavy Accra traffic and made my way to the bank to do my usual deposits. While I was completing the paperwork, the Relationship Manager approached me and asked that I should come to her office. There she told me about something called Stanford Seed, where they were looking for companies that could potentially be part of a 10-month entrepreneurial program in 2016. She had been approached by the organization to recommend some of the bank's business clients that matched a certain profile – companies that were well-established, with a turnover of over US$100,000 per year. She handed me an invitation card and said that I should go.

The event was being held at the Golden Tulip Hotel, a five-star location. I still only owned two pairs of trousers, so I found the best looking one and put it on and brushed my **scuffed** shoes for a bit of a shine. That night of the dinner, I joined a contingent of entrepreneurs from across West Africa to listen to the Stanford Seed faculty presentation. The Seed Transformation Program was geared towards businesses that had been around for longer than three years, and with revenue turnovers from the low hundred thousands, to in excess of ten million US dollars. I glanced around the banquet room and felt quite inferior when I compared myself to the well-dressed men and women seated at the tables, who all looked like they were doing very well in their respective fields. I decided to keep a low profile, to listen more than I spoke.

The more I heard, the more I wanted to be part of it – but I wondered how an entrepreneur like me without a proper office or even business set up would be considered. I knew that Stanford was a prestigious university in the US, and this was the first time that I learned they offered business growth programs to entrepreneurs in Africa. The faculty explained how the Seed program would give entrepreneurs like me the tools, skills, and mindsets they needed to scale and grow their businesses. The part I was most interested in was when they spoke about peer groups and coaching. I had already seen in my business life how much one could learn from the experiences of others. We were informed that the application process was competitive, with a screening system and shortlist, followed by an interview. When they mentioned how the CEO and management team would be evaluated, and that the companies they would choose needed to align with Seed's goal to make a positive global impact, I felt disheartened about Nissiguide's boot-strapped footprint in such a small part of the world.

Still, I left the Golden Tulip presentation, eager to apply – and when I finally got the news that Nissiguide had been accepted, I was so pleased that I didn't even care how I would have to manage my limited wardrobe day after day to show up and learn. The Seed program was beneficial in so many ways. First, as we sat in peer groups, I found out that no matter the size of the business, the entrepreneurs next to me were experiencing the same challenges that I was facing. I still felt like I was the small boy in shorts compared with the big boys of business in their expensive suits, yet knowing they were struggling too gave me the confidence to be a little more open. Soon I had befriended Temitope Louis Razack, the CEO of a trading company. We bonded over business stories, our Nigerian backgrounds, and shared values; we became business partners eventually and have a good friendship. I also met James Sagoe at the Seed program, the times we spoke during sessions, I had the sense he was genuinely interested in my growth and development. He would always seek me out and ask how business was going, and if I started complaining he would encourage me to notice the good things.

When James was assigned as Nissiguide's business coach, I was elated and nervous, feeling that our business ambitions were low and that our business operations were a bit too humble. Our one-on-one Seed coaching session was approaching, and I nearly had a panic attack when James said he would be coming to our Nissiguide offices to do the coaching. You see, we were doing all our business from a storage room. There was no office set up, just an unfinished room with bare cement walls where we had crowded some makeshift tables and mismatched chairs. The night before the coaching session I couldn't sleep. In the morning, James arrived in his Mercedes, and I went to meet him and lead him back to our storage room, where we didn't even have a white board or flipchart. Do you know the most interesting thing? His facial expression stayed the same all the time – eager, open, and happy to be there with us. That man was amazing; he managed that small space where he couldn't even walk or turn around, and he delivered a training in simple, clear words. We asked questions; we learned. He transformed that storage room and I felt like he radiated with hope and energy – it was such a moving experience for me and my team.

With all the benefits we gained being part of the Stanford Seed Transformation program, that was one of the best. Stanford Seed was an equalizer. It let our small business have access to a man like James, whose seasoned expertise we would never have been able to afford on our own. Seed brought us into a new circle of influence. Somewhere in my youth there had been a lesson that when one lies down with dogs, you pick up fleas. Well with this Stanford program we were taken to a new place, standing in a room with giants of business, men and women who raised us high, who lifted our ambitions and directed us to ways that our business could scale and grow beyond what we had imagined. I was no longer on the ground in low places. I was soaring to new levels of possibility, and it felt very good.

With Seed, my entrepreneurial mindset was broadened to go beyond fixing problems that had occurred, and to scan my environment and spot potential problems that needed simple, doable solutions. We did a training session on design thinking, and it was one of the most profound lessons I learned in the program. Perhaps it was because I am naturally drawn to engineering, so to discover there is a design way to think, act, and interact with problems where you can create innovative products and services for customers was a tremendous mind shift. Looking back, I realized I had already used design thinking to create my niche market of customers. They were always my focus, and so finding ways to deliver their waste management services flexibly, according to what they needed, being willing to think differently from my competitors – that had been design thinking without me even knowing it.

I was fascinated with the insight that design worked in spaces where people didn't even know they had a problem to solve. Imagine, at some point in history, some person sat in an airport and watched hundreds of travelers carrying suitcases back and forth between flights and destinations, and said, let's put wheels on suitcases! Then someone else looked at suitcase handles and said, wouldn't it be great if the handle could move up and down. And what about people who make money out of thin air? I had a friend who designed a training course in safety, and he went out and told businesses they should be training their staff in safety principles. These businesses hadn't even thought about the need for such training, and he showed them the gap. He hired a venue, got people to pay for the course, and suddenly he was making money, and he had a repeat business idea.

Looking to the future, my path of design thinking was also stirring ideas for how Nissiguide could identify gaps and opportunities, especially with government and global organizations, to find resources that others could contribute for solutions. I started talking with peers and mentors about some of the big challenges I was seeing in sanitation and waste management. After Stanford Seed, it no longer felt ambitious to consider how to make clean living a part of every home, kiosk and business in Africa's growing urban areas, so that people and companies can easily turn waste into energy that will help fuel improvements in communities, and everyone can be part of the solution to ensure that Africa rids itself of sanitation and waste management problems for a better future.

I was especially intrigued by malaria being caused by mosquitoes in areas plagued by sanitation and waste challenges. Billions of dollars are spent on solutions to get rid of malaria-carrying mosquitoes with genetics and pesticides. Design thinking got me to the question: why don't we create communities where mosquitoes don't thrive, and people do? I could see an integrated solution – working at multiple levels to create cleaner living, better sanitation, and waste management in homes and communities. My mind shifted to how we could use community links and assets (social capital) to help people take action to "clean and green" their environments. Soon I was having conversations with my mentors about urban planning and dredging and waste flows, managing erosion, planting natural repellents, and how we could empower communities through job creation in waste management, sanitation, and mosquito abatement.

James Sagoe from Stanford Seed was one of the people who listened to my ideas, and one day he asked if I had given any thought to public health and exploring business growth and social impact. As I thought about these possibilities, I found myself recalling a lifetime ago where my mission had been solely oriented towards finding financial freedom so that I could secure my family's future. Yet this long journey had brought me to a new vantage point, one where I could see how solving problems and creating financial freedom could benefit other families and communities too. I took all these new ideas on board and began to shape a vision for a different kind of growth, and soon I was enrolled at Ensign University in the Eastern Region to complete a master's degree in public health.

14
And then Covid came

When Covid came, it was a game changer for many businesses. In Ghana, and indeed in West Africa, the pandemic arrived on muffled feet, with quiet whispers and occasional coughs. While the entire world came to a literal standstill, on the African continent, we all paused to see how the virus would affect our lives. Within months it became apparent that Covid would not have the same impact as it was having in Asia, Europe, and North America. Global health organizations speculated about causes for the virus being less deadly in Africa. Reasons ranged from the hot climate and low testing rates to the fact that Africa's billion plus population is young – with a median age of 19; less than 3 per cent of the people in Africa are older than 65. Ironically, perhaps the one thing Africa had in its favor was that we were used to dealing with deadly diseases.

From what I could see, the virus was not making people sick. Even those around me who tested positive, many of them were asymptomatic, and the medical cure being prescribed was plenty of Vitamin C with some extra zinc tablets if you could find them. We were blessed. Still, we all jumped on the fear bandwagon, wearing colorful masks, and washing hands for those who had access to water. You would drive in the poorest communities and see how at the roadside some aspiring young engineer had rigged up a wooden wash stand, with a water bottle dangling from a rope. The real impact on our lives was suffering from the global shut down, the ripple effect on our economies, and the consequences of donor aid being diverted to the Covid cause. Africans are resourceful, and soon everyone in government and business was looking for ways to benefit from Covid.

In our case, Nissiguide would come out on top of the pandemic crisis because of the freedom we had to make vital decisions. Waste management was still an essential service, and we were able to move about even when most others had switched off their vehicles. We made a rapid investment in newer, smaller trucks and parked the big compactor trucks. That saved on fuel costs. As diesel became more expensive, we shifted our collection schedules to maximize our routes, which was easier because Covid meant less traffic. Our clients also accepted a price increase, which they saw as justifiable in the light of the cost of diesel. People stayed home in their apartments and complexes, and that meant for landlords, there was always trash that had to be collected. By the time diesel prices dropped again, we kept our price increase in place. Less maintenance, more affordable vehicles, continuous collection, higher prices – these factors made Nissiguide profitable during Covid.

When we finally emerged from the pandemic (something that happened more rapidly in West Africa than in the rest of the world), we saw Nissiguide continue to grow, especially with clients who were expanding their real estate properties. And so, my problem-solver mind kept spinning, seeking new avenues for making revenue where control over cash and costs were better defined. That feeling of "just try" was stirring again. Fumigation and waste management were the bread and butter of the business, and all the while during Covid, I was beginning to see how to add new sandwich toppings to our business mix. As Covid faded from our lives, the building boom started in Ghana.

With many of our clients being in real estate, I was constantly watching construction progress across several building sites. Gradually I made time to become active as an observer, looking at designs, watching how various aspects of developing properties unfolded. My maintenance knowledge was useful, especially as I became more familiar with real estate management processes. Unconsciously I had been absorbing more and more about real estate development. And it seemed future-wise to explore putting money into real estate to store our disposable liquid assets and let inflation carry us through to the new business project forming in my head. One of the other benefits of Covid was that I spent more time at my home and each day as I looked around the property, I could see the potential for growth. At first, I planted vegetables and fruit trees, and as the ground started to yield produce, my mind turned to buildings that could bring an income. I knew that within a short time, I was going to branch into real estate development.

After Stanford Seed I had also expanded my life in new ways, especially around networking and building peer relationships. Covid slowed down big gatherings of social interaction, but there were still the small networking groups, such as the Rotary Club. In my mind's eye, when I signed up for Rotary, I had imagined an environment more like the Seed program, and at the outset I was somewhat disappointed with the level of engagement. I discovered that the focus was less on business and more about finding a good cause as a reason to do social outings. Don't get me wrong, I really did appreciate being able to go into the community and make a difference. But I hungered for deeper business connections and a stronger network of entrepreneurial-minded friends.

Slowly my circle of business friends started to emerge and strengthen. At Stanford Seed, I formed a lasting relationship with Temitope Razaq Louis, and we started working on joint venture ideas that would see us collaborating across Nigerian and Ghanaian borders. Through our connections and partnership, I met another man whose life story and example as a business leader would inspire me – Dr Princewill Omorogiuwa, the CEO of the Simon Page education brand. Princewill's vision of achieving the phenomenal in Africa resonated deeply, with his belief that our continent is filled with adaptable people who have untapped potential. From Rotary, I found Carl Maxwell Brew-Aidoo, the founder of the successful Arc Aura architects' group. Mr Nuamah also remained close, frequently inviting me to his home on a weekend for a hearty breakfast.

From all these friends and mentors, I saw the value of placing your family's wellbeing at the heart of your business activities. I would pay attention as they spoke of raising their children and planning well in advance that they would be able to attend international schools. I listened as they shared about family vacations each year that would be seen as a celebration of being together and benefiting from whatever wealth had been created through business. For all the years I was away from Nigeria and growing my businesses in Ghana, I had known that one day I would have a family of my own. Now, as I reached the milestone of my mid-thirties, I knew without doubt that I wished to settle down – and that if I wanted to maintain my path to freedom and prosperity, then choosing the right wife would be one of the most important decisions of my life.

Being marriage-minded drew me back to my vision of using the land that I owned to build a bigger family home. Yet as I drove around the developing suburbs of Accra, I kept seeing so many large unfinished mansions. Perhaps that Seed design thinking inspired me again because soon I was picturing how to maximize my land by building three or four smaller storied units on the property, like the condominiums and town homes I was seeing in newer housing developments. Carl, my architect friend, turned my building concepts into actual plans – in no time I was staring down at architectural blueprints and seeing my future in real estate development starting to take shape.

Yet the biggest change to my future would come from Mr Nuamah. One Sunday morning he invited me to his lovely home among the trees and gardens up near Tse Addo, and as we sat to talk, a beautiful young woman emerged from the house carrying breakfast trays for us. She smiled, we talked about her studies, and I said that I enjoyed her cooking. Her name was Gloria. Soon she would become my wife, and the mother of my two sons.

Having children has defined my life more clearly, because I am now seeing how everything I do has a future purpose for them. It is a future that is strongly rooted in the poverty and sacrifices of my past, and the power of connections and opportunities. My experience with Martin Holmström at Ocean Rig never left me, even long after our ways parted. I chose to give him the only and best honor I could give a man who had transformed my life because he saw me, and he believed in me. When my first son was born, I named him Martin Obinna Ike. And I pray that one day, with his life, he too will create opportunities for others to succeed by believing and investing in them. My second son too bears the name of men who have mentored and inspired me – he is called Prince-Nuamah Obi Ike.

The day we held the naming ceremony for my second son, I looked over to my mother Theresa Ijeoma where she sat like a queen, dressed in pure white, her head held high as she smiled over her grandchildren. I remembered the time she never spent any money on outfits for herself, instead choosing to put her children through school and keep food on the table. Much of who we are is where we come from, and I am grateful for her devotion and example as a mother and a businesswoman.

Life has shown me that our plans will not always follow the paths we intended. There will be obstacles, there will be failures, there will be lessons, there will be successes. I am not sure that life is as rewarding if you live without challenges. Nothing is ever certain – that is worth remembering. No matter what comes your way, if you keep your mind on your future, if you make sacrifices and invest in moving forward, you can overcome problems and discover opportunities. The key is to know what you want and what you are willing to sacrifice to get it – I chose financial freedom and a better future for my family.

Glossary

Colloquial references

- *Akawo* (also called *esusu* or *adashi*) – an informal savings club, where members make equal and regular contributions into a money pool, usually weekly, or monthly, and where each member receives the entire pool of funds at a scheduled interval.
- *Bola* – garbage, trash, litter.
- Cedi – the Ghana local currency was redenominated on 1 July 2007, and 10,000 cedis became equivalent to one Ghana cedi
- Garri – dry, granulated food substance made from the root of the cassava plant.
- Fufu – made from fermented cassava or yam, rolled into porridge-like balls, and served as an accompaniment with meals, especially soup.
- Kenkey – fermented cassava dough that is made into sour-tasting dumplings.
- *Koko* – a porridge-style paste made by mixing corn dough and hot water, sweetened with sugar.
- Lights – refers to having electricity.
- Sacked – refers to being evicted or being asked to leave.
- SSNIT (Social Security and National Insurance Trust) – a Public Trust that administers the pension scheme for Ghana's Basic National Social Security Pension Scheme and first tier of the contributory three-tier scheme for employers.
- Kenneth D. Smith, a philosopher and academic, committed his life to teaching and mentoring young Nigerians who attended the Government Comprehensive Secondary School in Borokiri. He passed away on 21 March 2024.

Recommended assignments

In his story, Ike talks about challenges operating in Ghana's emerging waste management sector. For your assignment, explore how the waste management industry in the USA has been an easy target for criminal groups such as the Mafia, who have notoriously pushed out competitors, rigged prices, and used garbage collection to further their goals.

References

Chan, K. W., & Mauborgne, R. A. (2005). *Blue Ocean Strategy*. Boston, MA: Harvard Business Review Press.

Hill, N. (1937). *Think and Grow Rich*. Napoleon Hill Foundation. Meriden, CT: The Ralston Society.

Index